Creativity and Contradiction

European Churches Since 1970

Randall S. Lindstrom, AIA
Foreword by Dr. Robert H. Schuller

The American Institute of Architects Press
Washington, D.C.

The American Institute of Architects Press
1735 New York Avenue, N.W., Washington, D.C. 20006.

Printed in Italy by Amilcare Pizzi Arti Grafiche, S.p.A., Milan.

90   89   88   7   6   5   4   3   2   1

Library of Congress Cataloging in Publication Data
Lindstrom, Randall S.
    Creativity and contradiction : European churches since 1970 /
Randall S. Lindstrom ; foreword by Robert H. Schuller.
        p.   cm.
    Bibliography: p.
    Includes index.
    ISBN 0-913962-89-9 : $32.95 (est.)
    1. Church architecture—Europe. 2. Architecture, Modern—20th
century—Europe.   I. Title.
NA5458.L56 1987   87-27074
726′.5′094—dc19   CIP

Designed by Meadows & Wiser, Washington, D.C.
Composed in Bembo by Unicorn Graphics, Washington, D.C.

*Dust jacket and frontispiece. Interior
and exterior of the Wallfahrtskirche
Maria, Königin des Friedens,
Neviges, West Germany.*

For my parents

Foreword

I've said it many times: "Faith is . . . combining contradictions creatively." That's also a good definition of architecture! When it comes to religious architecture, the contradictions can be among the most intriguing and the combinations among the most creative. In this book, you'll read of a new Roman Catholic church, built in Norway for a Vietnamese parish! You'll see a new Ismaili Religious Centre planted in the heart of London! You'll discover what happens when a Scandinavian Lutheran Church is designed by a Hindu Indian architect! There are big churches in small villages, small churches in big cities and new religious facilities being shared by Protestants and Catholics. Contradictions? Yes, but combined creatively, they are really quite harmonious.

The author's interest in architecture and religion is well known to me. We first met in 1983 when he invited me to speak about my experiences in architecture to a public assembly in Rockford, Illinois. His investigation, presented in this book, is unique. It's neither a travelogue nor a catalogue, but a fascinating written and graphic exploration of the forces affecting new church design in Europe. By daring to become an adventurer and daring to explore, Mr. Lindstrom presents an opportunity for readers of this book to step out of our immediate environment and see how others express their faith through the design of spaces for worship. "Faith is . . . perceiving the worlds around you."

Triumph can come from tragedy. The tragedy in Europe is the low ebb of religious interest there. But the triumph I discovered in this book is that many of Europe's churchbuilders—architects, clergymen and laymen—are still producing new churches that are inspiring and appropriate to their context. As a client of the famed architect Richard Neutra, I came to believe very strongly in his contention that buildings should be designed to envelop human emotions in healthy, positive surroundings. Not all of Europe's new churches would meet Neutra's criteria, and each reader will find examples that inspire, and some that won't. But isn't it great that we have the opportunity to observe and understand the differences around us? "Faith is . . . adapting yourself to the unfamiliar."

I never wanted to build the Crystal Cathedral! I hated the thought of having to raise the money. But faith and positive thinking met the challenge and we dedicated the cathedral debt-free. Still, those of you who understand, as I do, the anxieties of a capital campaign will find the markedly different sources of funding for church construction in Europe to be an interesting, if controversial, alternative—unknown to most Americans. The European method of funding new church buildings is just one of the exciting discoveries awaiting readers of this book. As you travel through these pages and visit some seventy churches in ten countries, you'll find insight, impressions, images and contradictions that open a treasure box of undiscovered values. "Faith is . . . delighting in discovery."

Dr. Robert H. Schuller

Dr. Schuller is the founder and senior minister of the Crystal Cathedral in Garden Grove, California. In 1986–87, he served as public member of the Board of Directors of the American Institute of Architects. Over the past 30 years his ministry has expanded from his first "walk-in/drive-in" church designed by Richard Neutra, FAIA, to the weekly "Hour of Power" televised program, broadcast from the acclaimed all-glass Crystal Cathedral designed by Philip C. Johnson, FAIA, with John Burgee, FAIA. Dr. Schuller has written more than 20 books, including the best-selling Tough Times Never Last, But Tough People Do.

Introduction

"You should study the ancient cathedrals," barked Finnish architect Tide Huesser. "They were built when people still believed in God!" I sat, somewhat stunned, in the Helsinki, Finland, office of internationally known architect Alvar Aalto—eight years after Aalto's death—as Huesser, a protégé and colleague of Aalto, sternly continued: "Today, churches are just aesthetics, built to create jobs and spend church-tax monies."

I had come to this meeting at Aalto's office early in my four-month investigation of Europe's *new* churches, primarily those built since 1970. I had just explained my purpose and itinerary to Huesser. His response suddenly gave me cause for doubt. Had Europe abandoned its religious roots just as America was experiencing a religious revival? Could church and state in Europe be so interrelated as to permit a church-tax levy?

Although Huesser was unaware of it, his startling comments foreshadowed and strengthened the purpose of my research. Everywhere I went, I found doubts about the health of religion in Europe. I found church construction artificially resuscitated by mandatory government-imposed tax revenues collected from the populace. And throughout Western Europe, I found new church design creative and refreshing on one hand, while, on the other, torn between the influences of European history and American design trends. My itinerary included on-site documentation of more than 70 new churches and interviews with some 25 architects and an equal number of clergy. I traveled over 25,000 kilometers by car, in ten countries, from Finland to Italy and from England to Austria. Not all European countries are represented in this book, however; time and geography required that I direct my investigation where new church construction has been most prolific. Despite the important contributions in the arena of new churches made by countries such as Belgium, France, and Spain, the absence of a church tax has diminished the frequency of those contributions. And Eastern Europe has had neither the economic resources nor the political freedom to pursue any significant program of new church construction, although a recent flurry of construction in Poland may indicate a need and desire for new churches behind the Iron Curtain.

At each location I did visit, I sought to identify major liturgical, economic, and architectural forces affecting the design of new churches in Europe. In the interest of finding better solutions to our own needs by examining the work of others—and for the sheer joy of discovery—this book offers an exploration of those forces.

An Intellectual Battle
Over "Just One God"

Things happen fast in America. Within one short decade, the world saw Americans caught up in their past while reading Alex Haley's *Roots* (or watching the miniseries on TV), and then captivated by their future as prophesied by John Naisbitt in *Megatrends*. Europe moves more slowly, often with pronounced tensions between past and future. Protective of its rich heritage and increasingly infiltrated by the "progress" of a modern world, it is a continent of contrasts. Protestants and Catholics, for example, continue their bloody battle in Northern Ireland, while in Kettwig, West Germany, and Steinhausen, Switzerland, they can be found sharing new joint church facilities. And in West Sussex, England, Protestants frequently use a Catholic convent as a retreat and conference center. Despite a liberal inclination toward church buildings that are more inviting and less mysterious, many examples of new church architecture demonstrate an unmistakably conservative longing for tradition. Church attendance is on the decline, but new construction continues, with the church often taking on such additional secular roles as concert hall and neighborhood tavern. A Stuttgart architect sees religion—and church design—as victims of what is strictly an intellectual battle, because he ecumenically believes that in the final analysis there is "just one God."

Chapel at Priory of Our Lady of Good Counsel, West Sussex, England.

Protestant or Catholic: What's the difference?

Opposite. According to the architect, triangles are intellectual and, therefore, uniquely Protestant. Kirche St. Andreas, Reutlingen, West Germany.

"The dome is an emotional form"— but is it necessarily Catholic? Kirche Der Gute Hirte, Friedrichshafen-Nord, West Germany.

Stuttgart architect Wilfried Beck-Erlang contends that Catholics can be characterized as having historically been poetic, artistic, and emotional, while Protestants have been intellectual. He notes that Martin Luther was an intellect, and describes the differences between Protestants and Catholics as being of the mind, not of the soul. With many churches to his credit, the successful West German architect believes his own designs have mirrored the development of the Catholic church in recent decades. In 1962, Beck-Erlang designed the Kirche Der Gute Hirte in Friedrichshafen, using soft, rounded, essentially domelike roof forms because to him the dome is a Catholic form. "Like the grottos and caves where man first lived, and like the Mother's womb [a reference to Mary], the dome is an emotional form. Triangles are intellectual," says Beck-Erlang. Yet in 1969, when Beck-Erlang (himself a Catholic) entered a competition to design the new Catholic Kirche St. An-

"You've designed a Protestant church for us. That's what we Catholics need today!" Kirche St. Andreas, Reutlingen, West Germany.

dreas in Reutlingen, West Germany, he submitted a solution that featured not a dome but a dramatic, triangular form—one that the designer thought probably would not win. To his surprise, the committee selected his entry. At their first meeting, they congratulated him, saying, "You've designed a Protestant church for us. That's what we Catholics need today!" Whether by accident or design, Beck-Erlang profited from the ecumenical movement that is bringing Protestants and Catholics closer together.

Attempts to design ecumenical worship spaces can be fraught with risk. Success and failure can be achieved on the same project. In a design competition for the new Holy Innocents Catholic Church at Orpington, Kent (a relatively small city outside London, in the English equivalent of the Silicon Valley), a Protestant architect, Dr. Michael Blee of Lewes, England, submitted an exciting, efficient, and cost-effective solution. He not only won the competition, but also received widespread publicity in Great Britain and on the European continent. Acknowledging its architectural merit, the priests at Holy Innocents nonetheless complain that the new Catholic church is "too Protestant." They point to a crowded sanctuary (*chancel* to the Protestants) that provides no communion rails, a tabernacle obscured by columns that support the roof, and pews spaced so closely that kneeling is virtually prohibited. The architect counters by citing budget cuts and required space reductions that took place after design was complete. Holy Innocents' award-winning design is a successful outgrowth of the ecumenical trend among Protestants and Catholics, but it may be too aggressive in its diminution of the liturgical differences that remain.

Protestants and Catholics joined to build this ecumenical religious center. Filialkirche St. Matthias und Evangelisches Gemeindezentrum, Kettwig, West Germany.

An award-winning church with features that are "too Protestant." Holy Innocents Catholic Church, Orpington, Great Britain.

19

Gathering around: A plan for worship

Technology, communications, politics, and the natural evolution of history may have brought about the ecumenical trend of recent decades, but Vatican Council II in 1964 accelerated the process. One of the most noticeable earmarks of that trend is the nearly universal acceptance of the gathered-around, or fan, seating arrangement in both Catholic and Protestant churches in Europe and the United States. The development of worship seating plans in the postwar and post–Vatican Council II period can be traced in almost any community. New churches in the 1950s were, more often than not, continuations of style past, featuring axial, A-frame structures and classical, nave-style seating plans with a center aisle and usually equal sections of pews aligned perpendicular to the aisle. Then changes began to occur. Pews were canted to create a visual sense of "gathering around." In Catholic churches, the altar was pulled away from the reredos wall and turned around to face the assembled congregation, with the parishioners embraced as participants in the worship service. As organized religion became concerned less with ceremony and more with teaching, both Protestant and Catholic churches began to accept and employ the fan-shaped, or half-circle, seating arrangement. Some church architects even designed worship spaces "in-the-round." Among the most noteworthy examples is the North Christian Church in Columbus, Indiana, by architect Eero Saarinen—but churches like Saarinen's are more the exception than the rule. Symmetrical and asymmetrical versions of gathered-around seating continue to be the most widely accepted Christian church plans of the late 20th century.

The idea of gathering around for worship is not a new one. It was developed neither in the United States nor in Europe, nor as a result of Vatican Council II. Christ was a teacher who gathered his flock around Him. Archaeological evidence supports the notion that the earliest Christian churches employed an informal, gathered-around plan. In fact, seating was almost never present in early Christian worship spaces. How then did the traditional nave plan become so much a part of both Protestant and Catholic churches? The answer is a lesson in early real estate supply and demand.

When Christianity was legitimized in 313 A.D., Christians had little choice but to take over structures that were available— often meeting halls and basilicas that, among other uses, had served as rooms for the worship of Rome's divine emperors. This turn of real estate history was to affect church design for another 1,600 years and beyond. Elongated rectangular rooms had been built by

With a circular space come lack of orientation and acoustical challenges that can be insurmountable. Kirche St. Kilian, Paderborn, West Germany.

Communion rails placed behind the
altar require communicants to face the
congregation. Sædden Kirke, Esbjerg,
Denmark.

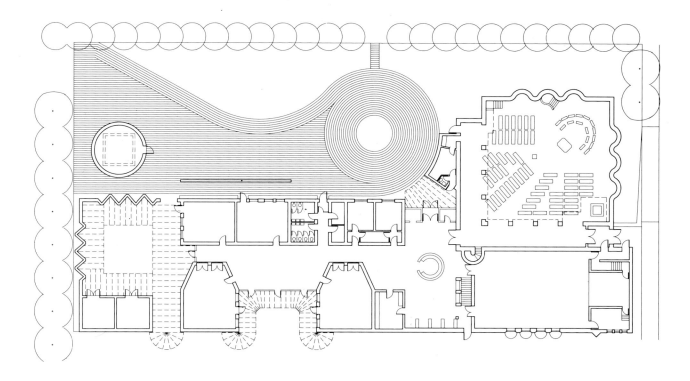

the emperors to instill an image of authority and worship. People were admitted at one end of the room to bring gifts to the emperor, who was seated on an elevated platform at the opposite end. This two-poled arrangement was adopted and used throughout the Middle Ages in conjunction with the liturgy of the Catholic church. As the great cathedrals were built, variations of the same plan were used, having become integral with the act of worship. Despite Martin Luther and the Reformation, the plan persisted, even into recent times, with displays of liturgical splendor that often had (and have) more to do with architecture and art than with worship.

Architects Inger and Johannes Exner, a Danish husband-and-wife team, believe that many of today's churches are still products of the Middle Ages. They cite architects and church clients who subconsciously design new structures according to the traditional, two-poled, elongated plan. According to them, their first church, built for an Evangelical Lutheran congregation in 1963, is a "Catholic" church because of its traditional nave seating pattern, its axial gabled roof form, and its symmetrical placement of the altar on an elevated platform, which requires the pastor at the altar to face away from the congregation. By contrast, as early as 1962, West German architect Fritz Hierl, in the design of the new Catholic Filialkirche

A revolutionary plan in 1978, but consistent with early Christian practices. Sædden Kirke, Esbjerg, Denmark.

St. George for the village of Grossweil, had already canted pews in a gathered-around arrangement and placed the altar away from the reredos wall so the priest could face the congregation. These features were somewhat revolutionary in 1962, but they foreshadowed what would become the norm after Vatican Council II.

Sixteen years later, the Exners started a revolution of their own with the design of the Sædden Kirke in Esbjerg, Denmark, which places the communion rails behind the altar, requiring communicants to face their neighbors, relatives, and peers in the congregation. Exner explains that, in early Christian services, bread was distributed but not consumed until after the service, when worshipers would gather around to share not only the bread but also their thoughts and emotions. When circumstances prevented the use of a building, early Christians would often gather in a grove of trees for worship and communion. In an architectural gesture to history, England's Michael Blee designed a church in 1963 at Isleworth (on the Thames River near London) with four structural columns supporting inverted wooden pyramids that make up the roof. The forms, he explains, are meant to symbolize four trees and recall the groves that served as churches for early Christians. Ironically, the seating is not gathered around but arranged in traditional nave style.

Treelike columns and roof recall the groves that served as churches for early Christians. Isleworth Parish Church, Isleworth, Great Britain.

Symbolism: The tools of worship

Symbolism—in architecture, art, and furnishings—may be the most important aspect of new European church design. In many instances, symbolism is all that distinguishes the new Protestant and Catholic churches in Europe. As might be expected, however, symbolism can be abstract, intellectual, and often contradictory. At the 1962 Catholic church in Grossweil, West Germany, architect Hierl installed a cross depicting a risen Christ—a symbol more widely employed in the Protestant church—instead of a crucifix. Yet in Protestant-dominated Finland, the Malmin Kirkko (1981), near Helsinki, features a traditional crucifix depicting Christ suffering on the cross.

A risen Christ, canted pews, and reversed altar in Catholic worship as early as 1962. Catholic Filialkirche St. George, Grossweil, West Germany.

Architect Helge Hjertholm of Bergen, Norway, has strong feelings about the cross as a symbol. He believes that the primary symbol of a church should not focus exclusively on the most painful moment in Christ's life, and that Christ's teachings offer many

meaningful experiences that Christians should recall. At the Søreide Kirke near Bergen, Hjertholm designed the ecclesiastical art form that hangs over the altar; neither cross nor crucifix, it is a metal sculpture that depicts molten clay (symbolizing creation), flaming hearts (symbolizing love), doves of peace (radiating to the four corners of the earth), a golden serpent (symbolizing the ever-present temptation of the Devil), and, at the center, a risen Christ. Hjertholm believes that, all too often, religion becomes a private club with special words and symbols that only club members can recognize. According to Hjertholm, Christ used simple symbolism in His teachings, not abstract notions that only intellects would understand. Therefore, in his architecture, Hjertholm prefers to use simple symbols.

A traditional crucifix in Protestant worship as late as 1981. Malmin Kirkko, Malmi (Helsinki), Finland.

Sacrifice and sacrament

Helge Hjertholm notes that "Christ was not an emperor," and says that pastors and priests "are not our emperors today." So he refuses to elevate the altar, keeping it instead on the same floor as the congregation. His architecture attempts to break down all barriers between clergy and laypeople. Even the roof of his Søreide Kirke has meaning: Each of the four "hips" in the pyramidal roof form are articulated by skylights. Hjertholm suggests that these four linear skylights, all rising to the same focus, are a reminder that "there are many ways to come to Christ, from the four corners of the world." At the Gug Kirke near Ålborg, Denmark, Inger and Johannes Exner elevated the altar and placed it off-center. But with clever and meaningful symbolism, the Gug altar is a square, four-legged, concrete table featuring twelve blue and white Danish china plates embedded in its top, uniquely recalling the Last Supper and avoiding the explicit connotation of sacrifice often associated with traditional altars.

The fundamental theological question about the central appointment of the church remains as unresolved in Europe as it does in America: Is it to be an altar or table? Dr. Richard Lischer, assistant professor of homiletics at Duke University Divinity School, observes that at the "table" there is bread, wine, and conviviality, while at the "altar" there is body, blood, carnage, and death. Both symbols can be argued to be appropriate because, in Christianity, the ultimate sacrifice makes communion possible. In Europe, both symbols are employed in a variety of styles—from sacrificial altars to casketlike monoliths to simple wooden dining tables.

Above. Sacrifice is clearly symbolized by a monolithic stone altar. Kirche St. Bonifatius, Lippstadt, West Germany.

Opposite. Square concrete table recalls the Last Supper and avoids connotation of sacrifice. Gug Kirke, Ålborg, Denmark.

Furniture aside, German architect Manfred Ludes says that the geometry of a church should stem from the altar, with the greatest height and light focused over the altar. Indeed, in most of Europe's contemporary churches, this precept is followed with apparent intention. At the Ristin Kirkko in Lahti, Finland, however, architect Alvar Aalto located the low point of a huge sloping roof directly over the altar, with the greatest height occurring above the congregation. One of Aalto's colleagues attempts an explanation by suggesting that Aalto was not very religious and may have believed that mankind is more important than religious ceremony. At a less philosophical level, it may simply be that Aalto, who was not unfamiliar with theater design, knew that a megaphone shape produces favorable acoustics.

Pulpit and pew

Seldom in Europe is the pulpit the center of attention that it is in many Protestant churches in the United States. Fundamentalist preaching churches are simply not a European phenomenon. In Europe, the pulpit is more commonly placed where tradition would have it, to one side of the altar. Architect Pekka Pitkänen of Turku, Finland, notes that in his Protestant-dominated country the altar is theologically more important than the pulpit, but his observation goes beyond Finland and is generally true of Catholic and Protestant churches throughout Western Europe. Pitkänen also observes that Finnish churches usually feature pews because, with so much alternate sitting and standing, pews are better than chairs. While he may be correct from a functional standpoint, the new churches of Europe—including those in Scandinavia—demonstrate no clear preference for either. Pews and chairs alike are used extensively, in settings Catholic and Protestant, large and small.

Font and fount

The position of the baptismal font in Europe's contemporary worship spaces ranges widely; it may be a counterpoint to the pulpit, at the opposite side of the altar, or it may be completely absent. With rare exception, the preferred style of baptistry is that of a font, meant for ceremonial sprinkling rather than immersion or submersion (new churches in Europe are rarely associated with the Baptist denomination, although a new Baptist church and youth center in London were completed in 1987).

Fonts that exhibit restraint and simplicity are often the most

Placed to one side of altar, an unusual elevated pulpit with sounding board. Sædden Kirke, Esbjerg, Denmark.

Chiesa di Christo Risorto,
Lugano, Switzerland.

Like road markers, painted floor graphics all lead to the altar. Pfarrkirche St. Stephanus, Gescher-Hochmoor, West Germany.

A circle of water in a square bowl. Baptismal font in the Gug Kirke, Ålborg, Denmark.

Opposite and above. The hills and mountains of western Norway inspired a truncated pyramidal roof form. Inside, an ecclesiastic sculpture symbolizes creation, love, peace, and temptation. Søreide Kirke, Bergen, Norway.

Mural of spring flowers behind baptismal font in the Gottsunda Kyrka, Uppsala, Sweden.

Above. Overstated abstract tree of life dominates small crucifix behind altar of the Catholic Chiesa di Christo Risorto, Lugano, Switzerland.

Opposite. Mosaic depicts symbolic images of the risen Christ, trees of life, and rainbow, but no cross. Gottsunda Kyrka, Uppsala, Sweden.

successful. At the Gug Kirke, the Exners designed an appropriate font that, like the altar in the same space, is a four-legged, concrete furnishing. The four corners of the square font turn up, forming a square bowl in which the water forms a perfect circle. Water drips steadily into the bowl and is released down a chain beneath the font to an exposed floor channel; the channel runs under an adjacent window to the outdoors, returning the water to the earth in a gravel dry-well. At the Gottsunda Kyrka in Uppsala, Sweden, a simple font is appropriately placed in front of a painted mural of spring flowers, subliminally and effectively symbolizing one's birth into Christianity upon baptism. But occasionally, exercises in design, form, and art seem to overshadow meaning; at the Catholic Kirche Bruder Klaus in Spiez, Switzerland, the font closely resembles a small hot tub.

Cross and crucifix

Nontraditional views of the cross and its place in a church are not uncommon among either architects or clergy in Europe. A Finnish architect, Pirkko Ilonen, installed no cross at the Vuosaari Kirkko near Helsinki. Instead, behind the altar, six cartoonlike drawings cast into a concrete wall depict major events in Christ's life, from birth to crucifixion. Ilonen hopes that each time worshipers visit the church they recall a different story about Christ—perhaps the one that is most meaningful to them at the time. Swiss architect Rino Tami, in the design of a new Catholic church in Lugano, Switzer-

Baptismal font or hot tub? Kirche Bruder Klaus, Spiez, Switzerland.

Drawings behind the altar depict
major events in Christ's life.
Vuosaari Kirkko, Helsinki, Finland.

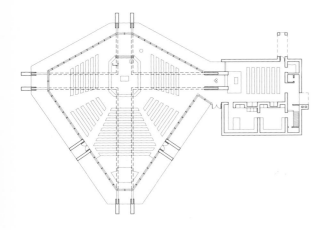

True to its name, Church of the Holy Cross, the floor plan is a modified cruciform. Moreover, four intersecting skylights make the cross a permanent architectural element, not a liturgical appointment. Katholische Kirchengemeinde Heiligkreuz, Altendorf-Ulfkotte, West Germany.

Opposite. The central symbol comprises diverse imagery—large wooden cross, tree, and "raven." Ravnsbjergkirken, Viby (Århus), Denmark.

land, purposely understated a small cross mounted on a wall near the altar, and overstated a huge relief in the concrete reredos wall, depicting an abstract tree of life. At the Catholic Kirchengemeinde Heiligkreuz in Altendorf-Ulfkotte, West Germany, the crucifix is not an appointment in the space but an integral part of the structure, formed by four intersecting bands of skylights in the roof overhead. The Gottsunda Kyrka in Uppsala, Sweden, by architect Carl Nyren, contains no permanent cross; on the prominent wall behind the altar is a huge, colorful mosaic of a living Christ, appearing to hover on a rainbow that bridges two trees of life. At the Østerås Kirke near Bergen, Norway, the traditionally symbolic Greek letters *alpha*, *omega*, *rho*, and *chi* form an untraditional cross executed in colored tile and copper behind the altar. And the cross is not the only nontraditional feature here: Østerås Kirke was designed for a Norwegian Evangelical Lutheran congregation by an Indian architect of the Hindu faith.

Wooden sculpture—large and almost oversized—becomes the central symbol at the Ravnsbjergkirken near Århus, Denmark. The powerful piece begins as a wooden cross but, with the addition of other wooden elements as "foliage," it also represents a tree of life. Natural light—symbolically promoting growth—floods the tree from a huge, adjacent rose window. This is effective symbolism, simultaneously depicting sacrifice, salvation, and hope, but on a sunny day the clear, round window admits so much light and creates so much contrast in the relatively dark worship space that the effect is distracting, if not uncomfortable. Suspended over the cross and tree is a wooden, birdlike figure—also very large—which, without explanation, could be interpreted to symbolize perhaps the dove of peace or, more likely, the community's namesake, the raven. (An outspoken member of another Lutheran church in the Århus area says the wooden bird at Ravnsbjergkirken "looks like a vulture." Clearly, America has no monopoly on diversity of public opinion and competing viewpoints.)

Of course, among all of these unusual, interesting, and exciting exercises in symbolism, one can also find the simplest and most straightforward examples. A rustic wooden cross—of the "old, rugged" variety—is the centerpiece of liturgical furnishings at the Gellerup Kirke, also near Århus, Denmark. Equally simple, the table, pulpit, and font complete a family of furnishings that is effective and appropriate in both functional and symbolic terms. But a common problem plagues the Gellerup Kirke: The organ is a mag-

Simple, functional furnishings, a rustic cross, a dominant organ, and a spotlight from heaven inside the Gellerup Kirke, Brabrand (Århus), Denmark.

nificent instrument that, like the organs in so many European churches, is overpowering in size. Placed in close proximity to the chancel, it inspires one to wonder whether the purpose of this church is to facilitate the worship of God or the worship of its organ. (If European church choirs were not so small—usually ten or fewer members—the visual dominance of music could be even greater.) Fortunately, on sunny days, God and the architect have combined efforts to cause a magnificent beam of morning light to strike the wall behind the chancel and terminate at the cross like a spotlight from heaven. When present, the light becomes an equally important liturgical element and, whether by accident or design, integrates the other furnishings of the Gellerup Kirke—including the organ—into a pleasing composition.

Instrument and monument

Another traditional symbol of liturgy, and one especially popular at contemporary Scandinavian churches, is the bell tower. The design of this exterior fixture, too, can become more of an exercise in art and form than meaningful symbolism. At the Gellerup Kirke, the bell tower is a fitting complement to the structure-dominated design of the church. Nonetheless, its form is more reminiscent of a fireman's training tower than of a campanile. At the Avedøre Kirke

in suburban Copenhagen, the streetside bell tower also serves as the main entrance to the church, as tradition often dictates. But this bell tower appears defensive—too defensive for those who would have a church say "welcome" to its visitors. The vision of a prison guard-tower springs too easily to mind.

Traditionally, the image of a European church is the image of its bell tower rising above the horizon, dominating the skyline of a village or a city. Today, in Europe as in America, those skylines are all too often dominated by industrial smokestacks or nuclear plant cooling towers. Not so at Viby, in suburban Århus, Denmark. There, with the power of form and size, the Ravnsbjergkirken rises above the horizon like a mountain. Dominating its exterior is a bell tower that is medieval and fortresslike in character. Actually rising no taller than the church itself, the bell tower, through careful design and articulation of form, is at once integral with the church but standing free of it. Architect Mads Møller of C. F. Møllers Tegnestue in Århus has created a massive and powerful church—a church that some might perceive as austere, but one that stirs the blood and arouses the emotions in a manner comparable to the experience of approaching Nôtre-Dame at Paris.

What about the musicality of these towers? A bell tower is of little value unless it speaks to the community and calls the congrega-

Structure-dominated design produces pleasing volume and effective natural light, but the bell tower, left, resembles a fireman's training tower. Gellerup Kirke, Brabrand (Århus), Denmark.

Streetside bell tower is appropriately placed, but its image seems defensive. Avedøre Kirke, Hvidovre, Denmark.

A chamber of reflectors in the bell tower controls the distribution of sound. Opstandelseskirken, Albertslund, Denmark.

tion to worship. With what voice should it call? According to the Exners, "The bell tower is an instrument, not a monument!" They suggest that a bell is most melodious when its sound reflects off other surfaces before reaching the ear. Just as the sounding board of a piano reflects the strike of the hammer on a string, an Exner bell tower never exposes its bells; instead, it places them in a chamber of reflectors designed to control the distribution of sound. Ironically, the Exners have designed several exciting and unique bell towers that could, indeed, be called monumental. Some appear to be unusually large at the base of the tower. But the massive scale derives from tradition: In Scandinavian churches, the room at the base of a bell tower often serves as the morgue in which a body is held until the funeral. The Exners readily admit that, for them, a bell tower is an opportunity to design for the sake of art, and they are not afraid to tell a client just that without apology. Their dictum: "If it's art, then say it's art!" The Exners are proud of, and motivated by, the art in architecture.

*Medieval and fortresslike, the bell
tower is integral with the church, yet
free of it. Ravnsbjergkirken, Viby
(Århus), Denmark.*

Clarity and clutter

Even the best of symbolism in the appointments of a church can be ineffective if the worship space suffers from visual clutter. No matter how complex its subject matter, a good photograph, painting, or sculpture needs a focus—something to which the eye is first drawn. The same is true of a church. Regardless of denomination, key issues—particularly whether the altar, pulpit, cross, organ, or choir is most important to the service—need to be addressed as intentional design decisions. If they are not, the results can be chaotic.

Examples of liturgical clutter can be found in new churches throughout Western Europe. At the Østenstad Kirke near Oslo, Norway, one enters the worship space to find an elevated altar, a large pulpit, a suspended sculptural cross, a wall-mounted tapestry, a stained glass window, a large pipe organ, and the roof structure itself—individually beautiful but all in the same cone of vision. Bright, uncontrolled daylight from behind the altar tends to silhouette many of the appointments. As a result, much of the symbolism is lost. Similarly, at the Avedøre Kirke near Copenhagen, Denmark, a fundamentally good worship space is cluttered with too many

Opposite. In Scandinavia, the room at the base of a bell tower is often the morgue. Sædden Kirke, Esbjerg, Denmark.

Above. Individually elegant interior furnishings, but all in the same cone of vision. Østenstad Kirke, Østenstad, Norway.

Owner-added tapestry, cross, and miniature sailing ship cause liturgical clutter. Avedøre Kirke, Hvidovre, Denmark.

47

Bold forms, understated furnishings, and controlled daylight masterfully focus attention on the altar of the Maria Krönungskirche, Zürich-Witikon, Switzerland.

Opposite. Clean, uncluttered, and ecumenical interior of the Katholische Kirche Zu Allen Heiligen, Berlebeck, West Germany.

visually competitive objects. The organ is placed such that almost nothing else could equal or outdo it in importance. Had only the table, communion rails, pulpit, and font been required, the arrangement of furnishings might have been visually acceptable. But the composition has been further complicated by such owner-added elements as an overly detailed tapestry behind the table, an undersized gold cross from the former church building (it simply *had* to be reused), and, floating overhead, a miniature Viking sailing ship, traditional Danish good luck charm and a symbol of the church as Christ's ship. Liturgical clutter!

There is no clutter in the work of Swiss architect Justus Dahinden. Using bold but simple forms, limited materials, understated furnishings, controlled daylight, and careful placement of the organ, he focuses unwavering attention on what is most important in the Catholic churches he designs—the altar. Dahinden's Maria Krönungskirche near Zürich and his Pfarrkirche St. Jakobus in Lindenholzhausen, West Germany, are among the finest examples of contemporary European church architecture. Interestingly, because of its striking simplicity and functional success, Dahinden's work supports the notion that the differences between Protestant and Catholic worship spaces are differences of the mind, not of the soul. Except for a few symbolic elements, his churches could serve either denomination. So could the modern, almost-Scandinavian design by German architect J. G. Hanke for the Catholic Kirche Zu Allen Heiligen at Berlebeck, West Germany. Its clean, uncluttered, and inspiring worship environment is both meaningful and ecumenical.

Traditional values

In Europe, as in the United States, Protestant church design and Catholic church design are converging. But church attendance, rising in America, continues to decline in Europe, and European churches are faced with the challenge of how to attract and keep their flocks. Some Europeans suggest traditional values—and traditional aesthetics—as the path toward rebuilding spirituality and church attendance. Despite a contemporary movement toward religious organizations and church buildings that are less mysterious and more friendly, Europe is steeped in religious tradition, and the desire to recall it does not go unsatisfied among the new churches of Europe. Architects in Denmark and Sweden have created serious, yet surprising, solutions to this need, and elsewhere in Europe many new structures share more than a coincidental kinship with the great cathedrals of the past. In Europe, as in this country, there always seems to be someone on the building committee who tells the architect, "We're not sure what we want, but it should look like a church." In America, that often suggests red brick, white trim, and the Colonial style. In Europe, it could suggest anything from Romanesque to Byzantine, Gothic, or Baroque!

How might an American church building committee react to an architect who suggested that the exterior of its new church be whitewashed with a thin, plasterlike material designed to start flaking off in about five years? (At the very least, church attorneys would probably begin rehearsing their opening remarks for the court battle to follow.) Sensing a desire for tradition—a longing for the maturity of an older building in a new structure—Denmark's Exners sold that idea to a sophisticated building committee in a suburb of Copenhagen. Their Opstandelseskirken was built of brick and then covered with plaster whitewash, a traditional building material. The plaster was supposed to begin peeling away in five years or so, exposing portions of brick and giving the building a mature, aged quality like so many older structures in Europe. The church was dedicated at Easter services in 1984. Just five months later—yes, months not years—the quest for tradition was satisfied. The plaster began to flake off and the church became "prematurely mature." Some who never knew of the architect's intentions say, "It looks like it needs a coat of paint." Others who understand the idea simply shrug and say, "We're getting used to it."

The congregation of Sankta Birgitta Kyrka in Kalmar, Sweden, shows more excitement about the traditional "roots" of its new church. Faced with an anonymous and uninteresting suburban site,

To lend an aged quality to the building, a plaster coat was designed to peel, exposing portions of the brick underneath. Opstandelseskirken, Albertslund, Denmark.

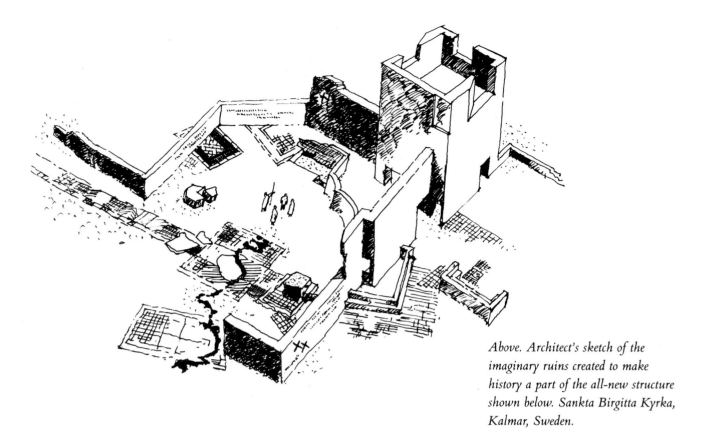

Above. Architect's sketch of the imaginary ruins created to make history a part of the all-new structure shown below. Sankta Birgitta Kyrka, Kalmar, Sweden.

architect Ove Hidemark of Stockholm called upon his knowledge of history, his imagination, and his skill to breathe both life and tradition into the project before him. Knowing that his new church would be compared to the circa-1600 cathedral in the city of Kalmar, he felt that, somehow, history had to be a part of the new church. So Hidemark imagined that his virgin site was actually the location of an old ruin that was "hiding a religious secret." He thought of his imagined ruins as having been a religious place, but not necessarily a church. First, he designed the "ruins"; then, like any responsible architect, he carefully designed a new church to surround and preserve the ruins. The tile floor of the new church, a pattern of varied colors and textures, suggests the remaining surface of what was once a "processional way." The floor is intentionally uneven, like the stone and brick floors of ancient cathedrals. Hidemark explains, "God never makes a perfectly flat surface; only man does that." The baptistry is located where Hidemark imagined the ruins of an ancient, holy well to be. Reinforcing that imagery is a "trickle" of blue ceramic tile that runs across the floor from under the new font. A bell tower was designed as part of the imaginary ruins and is left unfinished, "as ruins should be," says Hidemark. The new church is full of imagined history, and its painted ceiling, depicting a rainbow in a cloud-filled sky, is a gesture to the paintings on the church ceilings and domes of the Baroque era, Hidemark's favorite period in history. Today, the congregation and pastoral staff have expanded the imagined history that Hidemark brought to the

Opposite. Patterns of painted brick in varying planes give a mature, aged quality inside the new church. Opstandelseskirken, Albertslund, Denmark.

53

Right and opposite. An uneven floor, painted ceiling, new "antique" pews, and whitewashed walls fill the new church with imagined history. Below, floor plan of the Sankta Birgitta Kyrka, Kalmar, Sweden.

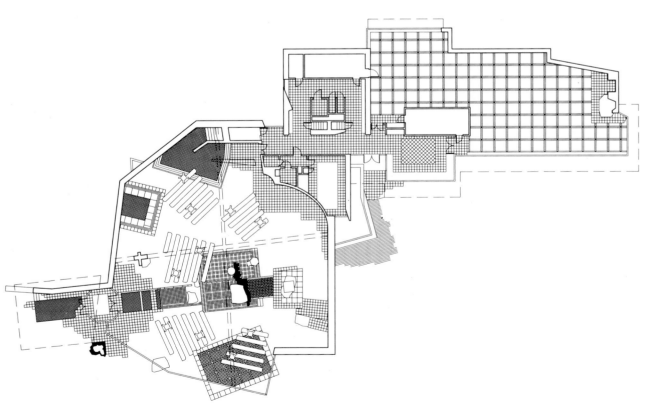

The pointed roof forms, often
mistakenly thought to have been
inspired by mountains, were meant
to recall the tents of pilgrims.
*Wallfahrtskirche Maria, Königin des
Friedens, Neviges, West Germany.*

project. When escorting visitors through the church, pastors and church members can be heard telling stories about the "ruins" that go far beyond the allusions to history and myth that the architect has suggested. With pride and satisfaction, Hidemark says, "History is behind you and ahead of you. When you build something, you have added your piece of history to the future."

Historically, religion has been used to explain mysteries and is itself based on elements of the supernatural, the unexplained, and the mysteries of life. Many people—especially in Europe, where tradition is so much a part of life—have been raised in the belief that a church building should embrace and express the mystery and authority of religion. To them, the ancient basilicas and cathedrals provide spiritual satisfaction and exemplify what a church should be. Today, in Europe, contemporary churches can be found that share an unmistakable kinship with ancient churches. Ironically,

Small, rural communities are often settings for the largest and least ecumenical churches, like this one in the Black Forest. Kirche St. Johannes der Täufer, Hornberg, West Germany.

these often enormous structures are usually located in small, rural, Catholic communities, where conservative religious beliefs and traditions are most deeply rooted. The concrete churches by Gottfried Böhm at Köln and Neviges, West Germany; by Rainer Disse at Hornberg, West Germany; and by Walter Förderer at Hérémence and Lichtensteig, Switzerland, are in their own manneristic ways awesome, mysterious, and nonecumenical. Their worship environments are characterized first by an overwhelming volume of space; second, by a sensual, if not actual, coldness; third, by an apparent darkness that prevents the entire structure from revealing itself; and fourth, by welcome rays of light that penetrate the darkness and often originate from unknown, or at least unseen, sources.

In parallel work, the Exners have produced new churches inspired by the Romanesque period of architecture, featuring closed, windowless worship spaces with solid brick walls and controlled daylighting. At the Sædden Kirke in Esbjerg, Denmark, the Exners suspended, at random heights, hundreds of individual car lamps, each on its own wire, creating an effect of "heavenly stars"—the architects' unique evocation of painted Byzantine domes that depict the heavens descending to man as he worships. Pastor Gertrud Bisgaard praises the design of the Sædden Kirke, but says she prefers the church's interior on bright, sunny days, when skylights illuminate the space and the starlike lamps can be turned off. According to Pastor Bisgaard, "the lights create such a powerful image that churchgoers leave the service only remembering the lights!" That, of course, could be as much a spiritual as an architectural problem.

In some cases, history is neither interpreted nor stylized but treated as a real and integral part of the project. At the Pfarrkirche St. Anna in Ascheberg-Davensberg, West Germany, architect Manfred Ludes preserved the village's religious history by saving and adding onto the 13th-century Gothic chapel there. And in Isleworth, England, a medieval bell tower, saved from the fire that destroyed the rest of a historic church, stands as a reminder of the town's religious heritage in the midst of a new church complex.

Medieval bell tower remains the centerpiece of a new church and forms a dramatic entryway for worship. Isleworth Parish Church, Isleworth, Great Britain.

*Addition to 13th-century chapel
forms a larger 20th-century church;
the Gothic structure serves as day
chapel and sacristy. Pfarrkirche
St. Anna, Ascheberg-Davensberg,
West Germany.*

Above. The plasticity and sculp-
tural opportunities of concrete
have permitted highly manneristic
expressions of form. Kirche in
Lichtensteig, Lichtensteig,
Switzerland.

Opposite. Cathedral-like scale can
still be found in many new European
churches, including the Pfarrkirche
Christi Auferstehung, Köln-Melaten,
West Germany.

Above. Heavenly stars—hundreds of suspended lamps—evoke Byzantine images of the heavens descending to man as he worships. Sædden Kirke, Esbjerg, Denmark.

Opposite. Overwhelming volume, sensual coldness, and welcome rays of light from unseen sources yield an unmistakable kinship with ancient cathedrals. Wallfahrtskirche Maria, Königin des Friedens, Neviges, West Germany.

Right. Concrete has replaced stone, but some worship spaces remain as awesome, mysterious, and nonecumenical as the ancient cathedrals. L'Église St. Nicolas d'Hérémence en Valais, Hérémence, Switzerland.

Above. Nontraditional tile and copper relief behind altar of Østerås Kirke, Baerum (Oslo), Norway.

Right. Restraint in new materials and forms successfully accommodates an ornate, historic altar. Pfarrkirche St. Jakobus, Limburg-Lindenholzhausen, West Germany.

Marketing the church

In hope of attracting and influencing larger numbers of people, Europe appears to have reluctantly accepted the movement toward liberalization and modernization of the Church while, at least in some sectors, still harboring desires for traditional values and traditional aesthetics. The declining influence of religion in Western Europe has caused expected soul-searching among Christians. Answers to the fundamental question, "What is a church?" come from both ends of the spectrum—from the traditional and conservative and the progressive and liberal.

What *is* a church? Is it sacred? Should it be used for secular purposes? Is it only for Sunday worship or has it a place in daily life? Should it boldly project a spirited form or unobtrusively provide simple meeting space?

In Denmark, church attendance statistics are fairly indicative of the general problem of declining church influence throughout Scandinavia and Europe. The suburban new town of Risskov, just outside Århus, has a population of 8,500. More than 8,000 are "members" of the government-sanctioned Evangelical Lutheran church. (Throughout Scandinavia, 90 to 98 percent of the population "belongs" to the state church.) On a typical Sunday morning, 50 to 100 people attend services at the town's new Ellevang Kirke, yet the sanctuary seats 250 and with overflow seating can accommodate nearly 400. The situation is a common one because, in Scandinavia, the church also serves as a community center—often a community's only social center, concert hall, or meeting room. The designers of the Ellevang Kirke did not overestimate the need for seating. They recognized that space was needed to accommodate not only the normally small attendance at church services but also the often large numbers attending concerts, lectures, and other secular programs that are held there almost weekly. The church is frequently filled to capacity for such events.

The Danish pattern of community behavior is common in Scandinavia and has led to new church designs dominated by the need for flexibility. Like most new churches in Scandinavia, the Ellevang Kirke features a large space adjacent to the sanctuary that can be opened to nearly double the seating capacity. It also features a movable pulpit, altar, and font to permit an unobstructed performance area, and a worship space designed as much for acoustic performance as for liturgy. Throughout Scandinavia, architects have employed the most creative methods to provide for flexibility and multipurpose use in new Protestant churches. At the Gug Kirke

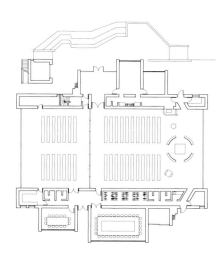

To accommodate both low attendance at church services and high attendance at other events, a movable partition nearly doubles the available assembly space. Ellevang Kirke, Risskov, Denmark.

As is common in Scandinavia, the
church also serves as community
center, and the exterior image usually
supports either function. Ellevang
Kirke, Risskov, Denmark.

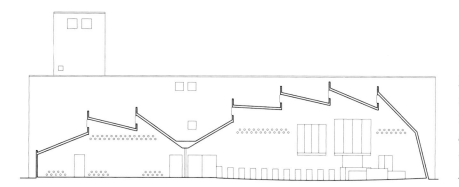

Dark green pews and the wood ceiling contrast sharply with painted white brick walls in an interior space designed as much for acoustics as for worship. Ellevang Kirke, Risskov, Denmark.

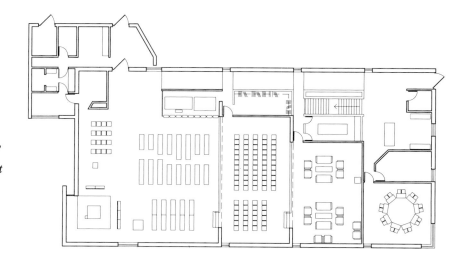

Flexible design features "telescoping" spaces behind the sanctuary. The first elevated space provides overflow seating or, when pews are reversed, can serve as a stage. Gug Kirke, Ålborg, Denmark.

*Reversible pews—like coach seats
on trains of years past—allow the
congregation to face either the chancel
or elevated "stage" space. Gug Kirke,
Ålborg, Denmark.*

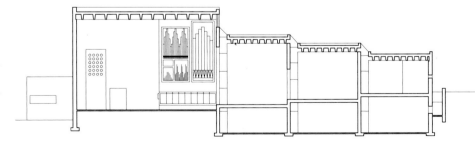

near Ålborg, Denmark, the Exners provided two additional expansion spaces behind the sanctuary, each elevated higher than the space in front so that sight lines to the chancel would remain satisfactory during seasonal religious services that require maximum seating capacity. Then, with daring ingenuity, they modeled the church pews after the coach seats on old trains. When a performance—secular or religious—requires an elevated platform, the pew-backs reverse themselves so that the seating faces away from the chancel and toward the first elevated overflow space, which then serves as a stage. With this remarkable flexibility, the Gug Kirke accommodates all of the functions required of it, whether as a church or community center.

Movable partitions allow classrooms surrounding the main worship space to be used as additional seating areas. Søreide Kirke, Bergen, Norway.

To meet similar multi-use expectations, almost every interior wall is movable at the Søreide Kirke near Bergen, Norway. Using a flat floor and movable partitions, architect Helge Hjertholm has designed a church that allows all of the classrooms sur-

rounding the main worship space to be used as additional seating areas during functions attracting large attendance. In the Netherlands, at Huizen, the Gereformeerde Kerk De Akker features similar flexibility, with dual-use spaces adjacent to the sanctuary and completely movable furnishings.

Few Catholic churches are being built in Scandinavia, but when they are built, far less flexibility is required. Attendance at Catholic services is fairly regular and predictable. And since the Catholic liturgy in these conservative churches suggests that God is actually present in the worship space, as manifested in the Host, the space itself is considered sacred and therefore an inappropriate setting for secular events.

In Germany, and generally throughout Europe south of Scandinavia, new church construction is more often Catholic than Protestant. West German architect Manfred Ludes notes that Catholicism is now an "intense way of life, not just worship services." Catholicism is so much a part of daily life that, in one instance at Dorsten, West Germany, Ludes found himself building a new church and cloister on a central-city pedestrian shopping street, immediately adjacent to the German equivalent of Woolworth's. According to Ludes, Catholics have been implementing a long overdue response to the need for ongoing weekly programs for retired people, women's groups, children's groups, and others. As a result, the Catholic church often finds itself in need of additional or new facilities. In contrast, Ludes describes the Protestant faith in Germany as being less intensive, attracting fewer people to church, and therefore needing new church facilities less often.

To an American, the ultimate in "public outreach" by a church is achieved in those German churches that also house neighborhood taverns. The new Catholic church at Dortmund is an example. Just inside the main doors, one may turn left to go to the sanctuary or right to enter a fully equipped *Gaststätte*, complete with bar, beer signs, and game tables. It is startling to Americans, but the natives to whom this is a way of life feel that the church should be a social center in every sense of the word. Perhaps theologian Johann Baptist Metz put it best when he jested that Germans "have a practical attachment to God, but a mystical attachment to beer!"

In contrast, most of the new churches in England seem to mirror the social and economic unrest of English society at large. In the fall of 1984, the English, hardened by lingering unemployment and a nationwide miners' strike, were cynical about religion. Many

*A new Catholic church and cloister
on a central-city pedestrian shopping
street. Franziskanerkloster, Dorsten,
West Germany.*

*Inside, a choice of spirits: to the left,
the church; to the right, a Gaststätte,
or public house. Gemeindezentrum
St. Aloysius, Dortmund-Derne,
West Germany.*

Above. Photograph taken in 1973 shows creativity in a modest project . . . but photograph taken ten years later, opposite, shows that time has been unkind. All Saints Church Centre, Windsor, Great Britain.

were surprised to learn that any new churches had been built in their country. In 1987, the Archbishop of Canterbury warned that "if a church listens only to tradition, it will speak only to itself." But regardless of its message, with only about 3 percent of the population regularly attending church, few in England are listening.

New English churches—both Catholic and Protestant— lack spirit in their exterior forms and their worship environments. Most appear to apologize for being churches. Many are little more than rectilinear, flat-ceilinged meeting rooms with applied religious symbols. It almost seems as though some of these new churches could, within minutes, be stripped of their furnishings and thus lose all religious identity.

Given the constraints of budget and current events, several architects have nonetheless made respectable efforts to provide good architecture. The new All Saints Church Centre at Windsor demonstrates creativity by architects Hutchison, Lock & Monk in a modest project. Photographs taken immediately after construction illustrate a simple but decent building. Ten years after completion, however, the building shows serious signs of wear and tear. Sadly, the same can be said for St. Margaret Church at East Twickenham and St. Elphege's Church at Wallington (both suburbs of London); Williams & Winkley Architects clearly demonstrated competence on the initial projects, but time—and, perhaps, changing values— have been unkind. Whether caused by poor construction, lack of maintenance, or vandalism, the condition of these buildings is an eerie reflection of the general condition of religion in England.

Dynamic roof forms point toward the heavens and show that spirituality can survive economic and social woes. Holy Innocents Catholic Church, Orpington, Great Britain.

In more recent projects, the church designs of architect Michael Blee demonstrate that current events are no reason to surrender design quality. Several of his projects prove that spirituality can survive social and economic woes. At Holy Innocents Catholic Church in Kent and the Priory of Our Lady of Good Counsel in West Sussex, Blee shows spirit and enthusiasm. But these projects are relatively new, and Holy Innocents has already experienced anti-Catholic vandalism.

Spirituality is surviving in Europe, but not with remarkable strength. Church construction survives as well—even thrives, to judge by the number and success of architectural solutions in several European countries. But the health of new church design and construction in Europe is due primarily to a life-support system—a government-imposed church tax. In many countries, church membership is virtually by conscription, and church construction almost entirely by government.

Opposite. St. Elphege's Church, Wallington, Great Britain.

Below. St. Margaret Church, Middlesex, Great Britain.

In Heaven (...and Europe) There Are No Fund Drives

Much to the amazement of an American who has been involved in a capital campaign to raise money for a new church building, *in Europe there are no fund drives.* Yet several European countries have seen a proliferation of new churches. The reason is a government-imposed income tax that goes to support church construction. Not every European country imposes such a tax, and where it is not imposed, church building is minimal; where it is imposed, construction continues and fund drives are virtually nonexistent. And were it not for the Constitution of the United States, church fund drives might be nonexistent in America, too.

Priory of Our Lady of Good Counsel, West Sussex, England.

For sale: Windows, pews, and bricks

Interestingly enough, an architect, Thomas Jefferson, is given credit for building the wall of separation between church and state in the United States. He and other shapers of the Constitution saw to it that there would be, in their new government, no federal "establishment of religion" that could tax the general public for its support. What evolved from this determination is a process of privately funded church procurement that is as curious to Europeans as Europe's church tax is to Americans.

One need not be a member of a church building committee to have seen in action the American process of fundraising for new church construction. In the late 1970s, the noted minister from Southern California, Dr. Robert H. Schuller, offered the more than 10,000 panes of glass in his then-proposed Crystal Cathedral for "sale" at $500 per pane. Within six months, every window had been sold. The buyers were from every state of the Union. At least five individuals, none of whom lived in California, each contributed $1 million or more to this project. To overcome skyrocketing costs (an original budget of $10 million had escalated to more than $20 million) and open the building debt-free, every seat in the Crystal Cathedral was "sold" to a full house of patrons who attended the cathedral's dedication concert. Today, a patron's name appears on each seat in the cathedral.

Though less elaborate and with less publicity, the fundraising process employed by countless thousands of churches across the country is similar. A building committee is formed, preliminary plans and costs are drafted, and then a campaign is mounted. Brochures, meetings, and personal contacts are employed to interest members in pledging a portion of their income or assets to the building project. Often, a professional fundraiser is hired to bring specialized expertise to the campaign. Although most churches cannot match the fundraising skills or the nationwide audience of followers that Dr. Schuller enjoys, churches all over America "sell" windows, bricks, pews, pulpits, and organs to those willing to "buy." Never in this process is the church allowed to clothe itself in the authority of the state by taxing its constituency. Concert and exhibition halls, municipal buildings, and schools may be built with tax monies, but not churches.

Taxation, but little representation

In Scandinavia, where church buildings also serve as secular social centers and concert halls, the Evangelical Lutheran Church is state-sanctioned and supported by almost every taxpaying citizen. The church tax in Scandinavia—and throughout Europe where the church tax exists—amounts to approximately 10 percent of each person's tax bill or, stated another way, between 3 percent and 5 percent of each person's annual income. Every citizen is taxed, although by disclaiming membership in the church and declaring yourself to be of another faith (or of no faith at all), you can be excused. Between 90 and 98 percent of the population accepts "membership" in the state church and dutifully pays. The other 2 to 10 percent avoid the tax, but they lose important benefits in doing so. If you're not a member and you've not paid the church tax, then don't ask the church to marry or bury you, or to baptize your children, because those are among the privileges of membership. This state of affairs makes it difficult to measure the depth of religious belief in Scandinavia today. Relatively few people regularly attend church, but fewer still are willing to relinquish church membership. Comedian Bob Hope once joked, "I've never belonged to any one faith because I don't want to blow the hereafter on a technicality." An understandable remark in America, but if Hope were a Scandinavian, he and most of his audience would likely all be Lutheran.

Among new Nordic churches, varying methods of collecting and distributing church-tax revenues have resulted in some apparent differences in design and quality of construction. In Denmark, the government's Ministry of Churches oversees and funds churches throughout the country. It uses tax funds not only to maintain and restore some 2,000 Gothic churches in Denmark, but also to construct new churches as they are needed. Monies are distributed to any locality (often a new town or a growing suburb of a larger city) with a proven need for a new church, without regard for the relative amount of tax revenue collected in that community. As a result, new churches in Denmark are of relatively consistent high quality, whether they are built in small or large, rich or poor communities. The Danish system of church-tax revenue collection and distribution is considered a model of applied socialism by the other Scandinavian countries. In Norway, Sweden, and Finland, the church tax is imposed by the federal government but collected and distributed within the local *kommunes* (equivalent to our counties). Since these districts vary in both population and comparative wealth, the monies available for new church construction vary accordingly. The process becomes highly political in Norway; in Finland, the poorest church communities can seek assistance from larger churches or, in some instances, from the federal government; in all three countries the quality of architecture differs from *kommune* to *kommune*. Yet, despite differences in methods of collecting and distributing the funds, the availability of church-tax proceeds has resulted in a wealth of new churches throughout Scandinavia. To the chagrin of clergy there, it has done little to boost church attendance.

The other nations of Western Europe are without a state church. Protestants and Catholics thrive with varying levels of status and popularity. In countries like France where no church tax is imposed, new religious structures are a rarity. But in West Germany, Switzerland, and Austria, a church tax is collected and new construction—although not as prolific as in Scandinavia—follows. After World War II, the Christian church in Germany, through the Christian Democrat Party, was successful in bargaining for a portion of tax proceeds from the new government. As in Scandinavia, the German church-tax rate today is between 3 and 5 percent of individual income. The federal government in Bonn collects and distributes tax revenue, which is split among Protestants and Catholics on the basis of their respective populations. German clergy consider the process fair; in the eyes of the tax-paying public, the church is wealthy. Switzerland imposes a church tax but collects and distributes tax monies through its local governments. As in Germany, both Protestants and Catholics share in the tax revenues. Churches in Austria suffer from the least effective church tax. Federal law mandates the tax, but collection is left to the local churches. As might be expected, the church is a poor bill collector, having little enforcement power. By claiming poverty or other extenuating circumstances, Austrians can avoid or evade the tax, leaving the church with few avenues of recourse. As a result, churches in Austria, regardless of denomination, are relatively poor, and church construction has nearly ceased.

Weakened by dwindling resources and powerless to tax, neither the Church of England nor any other faith enjoys much popularity in Great Britain today. In an interesting twist of history, the church tax from which our American forefathers fled is no longer a reality in England, and the absence of church-tax funds precludes most new church construction. In fact, England's most

Kirche St. Vital, Salzburg, Austria.

Ironically, the upstairs tenant is a government tax office, even though England no longer has a church tax. The design is functionally and fiscally satisfying, but much of the church's identity is lost. Christchurch United Reformed Church and Crown House Offices, Windsor, Great Britain.

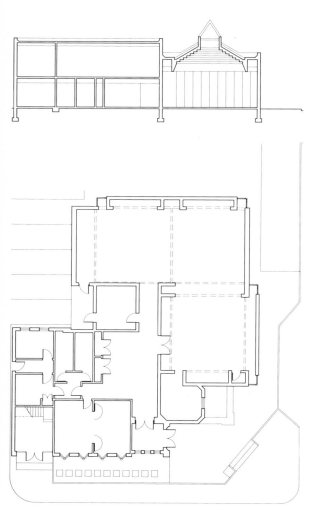

pressing religious issue now may be the fate of its "redundant" churches—churches that no longer serve a purpose, or that serve so few people as to be a financial burden. Medieval and Gothic churches (usually rural or in small towns) are being reincarnated, sometimes awkwardly, as apartments, restaurants, and offices. Many are falling victim to the wrecking ball.

One congregation in Windsor was faced with a dual dilemma: It could afford neither to maintain its Victorian church and grounds nor to construct and maintain a new church. With few alternatives available, the congregation sold all but a fraction of its center-city property to a commercial developer who razed the old church and erected a complex of office buildings on the site. The proceeds of the sale allowed the congregation to fund construction of a new church building. How would the new church be maintained? In a move that might be called entrepreneurial by some and just short of prostitution by others, the congregation built its new two-story church in a style similar to the neighboring office buildings, with its church rooms and worship space on the first floor and rental office space on the second. Continuing income from the "upstairs tenant" (ironically, a government tax office) now provides revenue to maintain the building. Windsor's United Reformed Church has survived, but in the process the community has lost a part of its Victorian heritage and the church itself has lost much of its identity.

All over Great Britain, congregations face similar financial concerns. Not only does England *not* impose a tax for the benefit of churches, its tax laws provide a disincentive for maintaining historic structures. A value-added tax is charged on repair work but not on new work, effectively penalizing historic rehabilitation and turning new church construction into a matter of crisis management—a matter of replacing older structures that have been allowed to deteriorate beyond repair.

The facts of life

Nowhere in Europe are new churches being built due to population growth or increased church attendance. In the United States, the opposite is true. Why, then, does church construction continue in Europe? In many areas of Scandinavia, the population still tends to be *decentralizing*—moving from the cities to new towns or suburbs—and the church is following. When a new town's population reaches 7,000 to 10,000, a new church is usually built. By contrast, many central European countries have built new churches in an effort to *centralize* and consolidate an expensive and unmanageable number of small, neighboring congregations into fewer, more economical religious centers. A new church in West Germany or Switzerland will often be built to serve several nearby villages, eliminating the need to support, maintain, and find clergy for three or four separate churches.

Church consolidation and, therefore, church construction in continental Europe are attributed to many factors. An alarming decline in the number of Catholic priests is a primary reason, reinforced in part by declining interest in religion. Other important reasons include World War II. Not only did the war destroy many churches, it resulted in the immigration of large numbers of East Europeans—most of them Catholics—into Western Europe, creating a need for even more churches. Later, the liberalized philosophies of Vatican Council II prompted both the renovation of older Catholic churches and the construction of new churches to accommodate a revised style of worship. And finally, the energy crisis of the 1970s demanded new, smaller, and more energy-efficient churches.

Europe's church tax has provided ample funds to satisfy most of the demographic, political, economic, and divine forces behind the postwar European boom in new churches. Few people today predict another decade of so much church construction, however; even the church tax has its limits. Nonetheless, several new churches are still on the drawing boards in Denmark, and in Oslo, Norway, at least one progressive professor of architecture is committed to producing a new generation of architects steeped in the latest architectural style, Postmodernism. Perhaps the Scandinavian church tax will prompt enough new construction for the Scandinavians to emerge as the leaders in Europe during a new period of architectural design.

Tales of Holy Jails

When God created the Garden of Eden, He didn't have to worry about architectural critics calling it trendy, old fashioned, or too modern. Nor did He have to compete with another architect to get the job. He had no neighbors to satisfy, no building codes to meet, no contracts to negotiate, and no building committees to approve or modify His plans. And no architect since has ever done more creating in six short days—though some have had a reputation for believing they could!

Today, the very complications that God was able to avoid are the challenges that make the building process exciting, rewarding, and sometimes particularly frustrating. In America and Europe, the process is similar. Architects, owners, building committees, neighbors, code officials, politicians, and architectural critics all share in the sometimes combative process of creating our built environment. On both sides of the Atlantic, we win a few and lose a few. In either case, we live with, and in, the results.

Sanctuary of the Katholische Kirche
Heiliggeist, Lemgo, West Germany

Fashion and public reaction

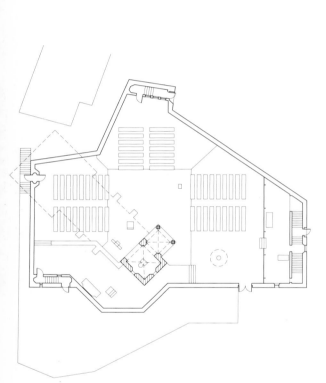

The new church surrounds the old, and a former porch becomes a sacristy. Kirche in Waldweiler, Waldweiler, West Germany.

In 1981, the Reverend John McNamara approached the edifice of a brand new church and muttered under his breath, "Thank God I don't have to serve in a building that looks like this!" Father McNamara had come to represent his neighboring parish at dedication services for the new Holy Innocents Catholic Church in Orpington, Kent, about 25 kilometers southeast of London. The church's dedication service had been appropriate enough, but its award-winning modern architecture was too much for Father McNamara. He returned to his parish content to have taken part in Holy Innocents' new beginning, but more delighted than ever with the traditional and historic roots of his own church building. His delight was not to last. One evening, less than a year later, Father McNamara answered his telephone to find the bishop of his diocese announcing that God was calling him to serve at another parish—Holy Innocents. Would a divine call overcome his architectural misgivings? It would, indeed. Today, the sign at the entrance to Holy Innocents Church still reads, "The Very Reverend Canon John McNamara, Priest."

Critical reaction to architecture probably accompanied the earliest attempt at organizing stones and timbers into shelter. But with the passing of each year, the lengthening perspective of history—not to mention the rapidity of advanced communications—affords a greater opportunity to compare, contrast, and criticize the fashions of architecture. Architecture critics, like their counterparts in *haute couture*, are quick to put labels on various styles and trends. Yet some of the most pointed criticism comes from laypeople, the end-users of all fashion and design. Danish architect Jørn Utzon won international acclaim for his design of the Opera House in Sydney, Australia, but in Bagsværd, Denmark (a suburb of his home town, Copenhagen), the townspeople say that his new church there "looks like a factory." The exterior does resemble a Midwest grain elevator; once inside, however, the visitor discovers a magnificent, uplifting worship environment that Utzon claims was inspired by clouds. Indeed, the interior appears to have a cumulous ceiling with the same kind of delightful, natural light reflected and diffused by those fluffy, white clouds. Soft, rounded concrete forms present a sharp contrast to the building's rigid, geometric exterior skin. Perhaps the contrast is intentional, but public reaction indicates it is hardly understood. In the small village of Waldweiler, West Germany, a new Catholic church with thick brick walls, a flat roof, small slit-windows, and a generally dark worship space is apparently seen by parishioners as being impenetrable and inescapable, because

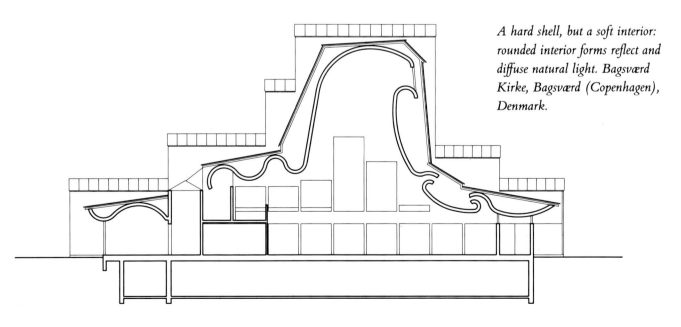

A hard shell, but a soft interior: rounded interior forms reflect and diffuse natural light. Bagsværd Kirke, Bagsværd (Copenhagen), Denmark.

Dubbed by residents the "Holy Jail," its interior provides abundant floor space but little volume. Kirche in Waldweiler, Waldweiler, West Germany.

area residents have dubbed it the "Holy Jail." Architect Heinz Bienefeld explains that the project's limited budget would not allow for both space *and* volume. Knowing the needs of the church and understanding that design is almost always compromise, Bienefeld used the available funds to achieve floor space, rather than volume. Public reaction aside, the result is quite intriguing. The modern brickwork appears to be ancient, and a portion of the former village church is left intact in its original position, becoming a sacristy for the new church built around it.

When reviewing a colleague's building project, architects often speculate, tongue in cheek, as to whether the designer's stated concept actually preceded and inspired the built result or evolved afterward as a rationalization—architecture's equivalent of the chicken-or-egg dilemma. This is particularly true when the curious idiosyncrasies of a project come to light. The wood-clad Gottsunda Kyrka in Uppsala, Sweden, is curiously painted a pinkish-red color. When asked what inspired that particular color, the Stockholm-based architect, Carl Nyren, said, "Red is the color of love. To be good Christians, people must love one another." Then, with a wry smile, he added, "Besides, red is my favorite color!"

94

Nearly every current style, trend, and movement in architecture can be found among the new churches of Europe. The Eidsvåg Kirke near Bergen, Norway, is typical of the International Style still favored by many architects. This Norwegian church is a crisp, all-white, cubic design, an exercise in masses and voids that rests like a jewel on a wooded site overlooking one of Bergen's picturesque fjords. From the same time period—the early 1970s—and also a product of the International Style is the Catholic Agatha Kirche in Buchrain, Switzerland, near Luzern. Unlike its Norwegian contemporary, however, the Buchrain church is far from colorless. Its surfaces are painted in primary colors—yellow ceiling, blue walls, red columns, red organ case, blue furniture—that are undeniably exciting but, to many, less than worshipful in appearance. Still, the design is a not unusual entry from the late Modern period.

On a wooded site, a monochromatic jewel that overlooks a picturesque fjord. Eidsvåg Kirke, Eidsvåg i Asane (Bergen), Norway.

The influence of the Pop-Art and Op-Art periods can frequently be seen in Europe's contemporary church architecture. In West Germany, architect J. G. Hanke, responsible for designing more than 20 Catholic churches in 25 years, has collaborated more than once with artists who employed bold colors and graphic patterns as accents on new churches. At the Catholic Kirche Heiliggeist in Lemgo, the concrete bell tower is ringed with a yellow band of paint; strokes of blue and white are painted on the exterior brick walls, announcing the entryways; and inside, painted chevrons of yellow, gold, red, and blue attract attention on a white brick wall behind the altar and on a similarly painted concrete crucifix. Even the structure contributes to the geometric expression. Exposed concrete roof-framing members run at a 45-degree angle to the square plan, forming a surprising and exciting interior ceiling texture. Outside, the same structural elements penetrate the brick wall, creating a modern-day frieze or cornice. The resulting structural decoration is integral with the building, a characteristic true to the Modern movement; the painted graphics are applied decoration, more typical of the Postmodern period.

Painted graphics emphasize both the bell tower and entryways, while concrete roof-framing members penetrate the exterior wall, creating a frieze. Katholische Kirche Heiliggeist, Lemgo, West Germany.

Hanke demonstrates a similar vocabulary of geometric, concrete sculpture and colorful painted graphics at the Catholic Kirche St. Josef in Bünde. Though pale in comparison to the work of Andy Warhol, Christo, and other more extreme artists, projects such as this one reflect the search for new expression that grew out of the anonymous International Style and foreshadowed the inevitable transition from Modern to Postmodern. The work of earlier architects has always been a powerful force affecting "new" design. The

*A new church that quietly fits
its setting in a Bavarian village.
Marienkirche, Benediktbeuern,
West Germany.*

Holy Innocents Catholic Church, Orpington, Great Britain.

Above. Exterior, which townspeople say "looks like a factory," encloses a magnificent, uplifting worship environment inspired by clouds. Bagsværd Kirke, Bagsværd (Copenhagen), Denmark.

Left. Its pinkish color symbolizes Christian love . . . and happens to be the architect's favorite. Gottsunda Kyrka, Uppsala, Sweden.

Above. Geometry and color attempt
to strengthen the liturgical focus.
Katholische Kirche Heiliggeist,
Lemgo, West Germany.

Opposite and left. A prism of
primary colors, but is it worshipful?
Agatha Kirche, Buchrain,
Switzerland.

Above. Rock walls, skylights, and copper-clad dome enclose the worship space. Temppeliaukion Kirkko, Helsinki, Finland.

Opposite. Wood, brick, and dramatic natural light form an inviting worship space. Islev Kirke, Rødovre, Denmark.

Above. Geometric sculpture and colorful painted graphics reflect the search for new expression growing out of the anonymous International Style. Kirche St. Joseph, Bünde, West Germany.

Right. Long after his death, the influence of Le Corbusier remains evident. Kirche St. Johannes der Täufer, Hornberg, West Germany.

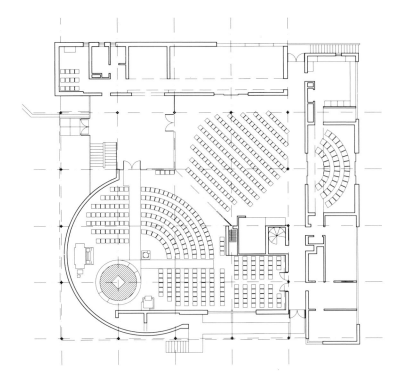

Floor plan of Bekkefaret Kirke,
Stavanger, Norway, is dominated
by a structural grid. A jungle gym
outside the church mirrors its exposed
structural steel skeleton. Bekkefaret
Kirke, Stavanger, Norway.

influence of Le Corbusier remains evident throughout Europe, years after his death. In the Black Forest village of Hornberg, a new church by architect Rainer Disse is unmistakably influenced by Corbu's work at Chandigarh, India. In Stavanger, Norway, the Bekkefaret Kirke by architects Per Amund Riseng and Jan Stensrud is dominated by a structural grid and exposed structural steel elements. Though not purely Miesian (after architect Ludwig Mies van der Rohe), this new church could be transplanted to downtown Chicago almost without notice. On Norway's west coast, in Haugesund, the same architects demonstrate their versatility: Though still structurally driven, the all-concrete form of the Rossabø Kirke is bold, spirited, and dynamic—and even though the pastor objects to the absence of an exterior cross, this design by Riseng and Stensrud unmistakably says "church."

At Innsbruck, Austria, architect Horst Herbert Parson readily acknowledges the influences of Japanese architecture and Frank Lloyd Wright—not an unlikely combination, since Wright himself was influenced by the Japanese. Parson's new church, in the residential area that once served as Innsbruck's Olympic Village, makes a strong and dramatically horizontal statement against the ragged vertical backdrop of the Austrian Alps. The effect is reminiscent of the creative contrast in Wright's design for the Marin County Civic Center in California. Inside the Pfarrzentrum Neu-Rum, a strikingly simple motif of black and white speaks of the Oriental influence in Parson's work.

In contrast to rectilinear and orderly solutions is the highly irregular and organic design of the cemetery chapel called Hochbauten Wald-Friedhof at Kirchheim-Teck, West Germany. Through-

Above. Horizontal counterpoint to the ragged, vertical backdrop of the Austrian Alps. Pfarrzentrum Neu-Rum, Innsbruck, Austria.

Right. A jagged, serpentine wall wraps the Hochbauten Wald-Friedhof, Kirchheim-Teck, West Germany.

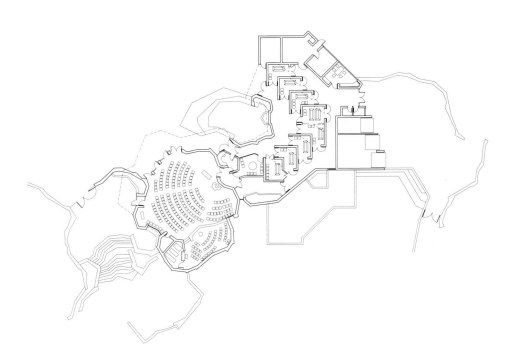

out most of the all-concrete building, architect P. M. Kaufmann departs from any structural ordering, instead wrapping a jagged, serpentine wall around the spaces, apparently in respectful deference to the irregular terrain of the site. The innovation, freedom, and ecologically sensitive design of this complex, too, echo the organic philosophy of Wright's Usonian projects.

Even the aesthetics of the early Space Age have had their effect on contemporary European church design. An American vis-

The all-concrete funeral chapel provides an appropriate environment and fits its rugged site. Hochbauten Wald-Friedhof, Kirchheim-Teck, West Germany.

Sitting on a rock outcropping in a neighborhood of five- and six-story walk-ups, the flat-domed church encloses an exciting interior that is suitable for worship and worthy of tourists' attention. Temppeliaukion Kirkko, Helsinki, Finland.

iting the Temppeliaukion Kirkko in Helsinki, Finland, might be tempted to label it a UFO. Like a giant spaceship, the circular, flat-domed church sits on a rock outcropping in the middle of a dense neighborhood of five- and six-story brick walk-ups as if it landed there. Its uniqueness has made this church a major tour attraction, drawing busloads of visitors every day. On sale inside are books, slides, and postcard views of the "unidentified Finnish object." The concept of utilizing and embracing the existing rock outcropping is admirable; to cover it with a Space Age dome seems an inappropriate contrast, but together the rock walls, skylights, and copper dome enclose an exciting environment, entirely suitable for worship and worthy of its visitors' attention.

Fitting the fabric of its London neighborhood, but speaking of another culture. Inside and out, integrity of detail and quality of materials prevail. The Ismaili Centre, London, Great Britain.

Sometimes, when history, culture, and religious beliefs are transplanted to foreign soil, no existing architectural style is appropriate. Such was the case when the Aga Kahn selected the Casson Conder Partnership, London architects, to design a new religious and cultural center for the Ismaili Muslim community in London. Ismailis belong to the Shia branch of Islam. They are generally a minority in the countries where they reside, and in London have few architectural monuments and precedents for an Ismaili religious and cultural center. The Casson Conder Partnership designed a building for the Ismailis that fits no category of architectural design. Instead, it uniquely and successfully satisfies the architects' stated goal that "it should be foremost a London building, not necessarily derivative from Islamic precedents, but in keeping with their mood." Practically within eyesight of Harrod's department store, the Ismaili Centre fits the fabric of its neighborhood but undeniably speaks of another culture. Completed in 1983, the design is accurately described in Great Britain's *Architectural Journal* as simultaneously "ancient and modern."

The rural vernacular of Litzelstetten, near Konstanz, West Germany, influenced architect Herbert Schaudt in the design of a new Catholic church for this small village. Recalling the roof forms of adjacent and nearby wooden barns, Schaudt sympathetically used the new church to surround the ancient church tower and apse that he was required to preserve. He did so with convincing results. All but trained eyes would assume the church to be a long-time landmark in the village. Schaudt cites a limited budget, a conservative parish, and a restricted site as the factors leading to his use of the village's traditional forms and materials. His only complaint is that local building and fire codes forced him to use larger wooden tim-

A rural vernacular of traditional forms and materials inspires the interior. Katholische Kirche der Gemeinde Litzelstetten, Konstanz-Litzelstetten, Switzerland.

Opposite. An uncluttered worship environment executed with elegant simplicity. Marienkirche, Benediktbeuern, West Germany.

bers than his aesthetic and historic senses preferred.

In the traditional Bavarian village of Benediktbeuern, the Marienkirche by architect Fritz Hierl is, like Schaudt's Litzelstetten church, a good neighbor. Though contemporary and fresh, Hierl's church quietly fits its setting. Traditional forms, executed with elegant simplicity, clearly speak of a village and its religious heritage. The Marienkirche is an old friend of the community, proof that not every new building needs to shout.

New churches must be good neighbors, not only for obvious social reasons but also because their neighbors-to-be can exert a powerful influence on design. In the United States, the property owners adjacent to and near a project can often muster the political power, through zoning ordinances, to dictate the height, size, and design of their proposed new neighbor—and, in many instances, the

power to prevent its construction altogether. In Europe, the power of the neighbor can be equally strong. At Rødovre, Denmark, Inger and Johannes Exner proposed a red brick church in a residential area of the city. The new Islev Kirke was to feature a small but uniquely designed bell tower. Under Danish tax laws, of course, most of the neighbors were members of the new church and thus could hardly object to its construction. But since few residents actually attended church, many found the prospect of being awakened by church bells every Sunday morning a disturbing one. In response to this neighborhood concern, the Exners modified the bell tower to funnel its sound upward, through several inverted brick cones, rather than send it outward toward the neighboring homes. The neighbors approved. But then, as construction neared completion and the bells were tested, the neighbors heard beautiful sounds emanating faintly from the tower. Having had no idea the tintinabulation would be so pleasant, they reversed their earlier complaint and asked the architects to do something so they could better hear the bells! At the last moment, "portholes" were cut into the side of the tower, and today the citizens of Rødovre happily rise on Sunday mornings to the sound of the Islev church bells.

Once skeptical neighbors now rise happily to the sound of bells emanating from "portholes" cut in the tower. Islev Kirke, Rødovre, Denmark.

Modern and Postmodern

Following the destruction wrought by World War II, Europe needed to build shelter quickly and economically. Style was seldom an issue. Cities were filled with bland and anonymous structures that provided shelter, but little more. In architectural circles, the postwar period marked the heyday of the Modern movement. Modernism's International Style was so generic and nonvernacular that New York, Paris, and Tokyo could embrace it as their own—a world united by a single architectural style. The International Style even pervaded the design of furnishings and lighting fixtures, but as Finnish architect Tide Huesser comments today, "Ultimately, one cannot save mankind with a chair or light." Indeed, the pendulum has swung and, according to professor Manfred Ludes of Dorsten, West Germany, the architectural profession in Europe is being roundly criticized for the *lack* of style that characterizes much of Europe's postwar construction.

Are Europe's Modernists turning to Postmodernism? Pose the question to European architects and you will receive as many different replies as there are architects, with each reply accompanied by anything from a skeptical smile to a hearty chuckle. The levity is a knee-jerk response to the image of Postmodernism that American

In Scandinavia, where darkness pervades so much of the winter, the design of light fixtures is almost an obsession. Henrikin Kirkko, Turku, Finland.

architectural journals have created—a rather narrow image defined by the often controversial and sometimes humorous approaches of such American architects as Michael Graves, Helmut Jahn, and Philip Johnson.

Actually, European architects have a much more serious view and a much broader definition of Postmodernism. Many see the movement as encompassing a wide range of styles, projects, and architects, all of which and all of whom share one common trait: a disregard for the rules, precepts, and edicts of Modernism. European architects have even suggested that such Modernists as Le Corbusier and Aalto were really the first Postmodernists. Corbu is given the dubious distinction because, at his church in Ronchamp, France, he "dishonestly" hid a steel structural system within forms that appear to be massive, sculpted concrete. Aalto is named because he is said to have discarded the fixed vocabulary of Modern rectilinear forms and was constantly experimenting with "new" forms and combinations of forms.

The Postmodern movement in Europe, at least as it relates to church design, is in its very early stages. When and if it develops, the movement may find its leaders in Norway, of all places. At the Oslo School of Architecture, several key faculty members are intently and energetically forwarding the Postmodernist cause. Professor Thomas Thiis-Evensen and his colleagues are committed to producing a generation of Norwegian architects who are well versed in the theories and principles of Postmodernism. The school is consciously instructing students to explore and implement Postmodern thought in their work. And so the Oslo school may find itself in the unlikely act of leading an architectural movement, a distinction that has more often gone to Finland or Denmark.

Thiis-Evensen claimed his first victory with the Postmodernist renovation of a church in Stavanger, Norway, as the new St. Svithun Katolske Kirke—a Catholic church for a predominantly Vietnamese parish. Among the four million inhabitants of Norway, only 15,000 to 20,000 are Catholic. But the oil industry on Norway's west coast has led to increased population there and, after the war in Vietnam, attracted Vietnamese and Cambodian emigrants to work on oil rigs in the North Sea. These refugees from Southeast Asia came from Catholic backgrounds and needed appropriate worship spaces. At St. Svithun's, Thiis-Evensen provided a traditionally Catholic environment, including an altar with baldachino and niches for statuary, but in neither classical nor Modern fashion.

Postmodern renovation of the Catholic St. Svithun Kirke, Stavanger, Norway.

114

*A typically "Modern" church from
1974. Kirche Bruder Konrad
Spexard, Gütersloh, West Germany.*

An altar with baldachino and niches for statuary—a traditional Catholic environment—for a Vietnamese parish in Norway. St. Svithun Kirke, Stavanger, Norway.

Design recalls forms of nearby wooden barns and incorporates ancient church tower and apse. Katholische Kirche der Gemeinde Litzelstetten, Konstanz-Litzelstetten, Switzerland.

Above. "Simultaneously ancient and modern." Ismaili Centre, London, Great Britain.

Right. The interior speaks of the influence of Frank Lloyd Wright and Japanese architecture. Pfarrzentrum Neu-Rum, Innsbruck, Austria.

Opposite. Sensitive 1983 alteration of an older structure defies categorization: "Postmodern" may be too extreme. Kirche St. Michael, Ummeln, West Germany.

Color, ornamentation, and decoration:
German Postmodernism? Herz-Jesu-
und-Maria-Sühnekirche,
Wigratzbad, West Germany.

A second victory came in the fall of 1984 when the conservative—and Modernist—school of architecture at Trondheim, Norway, invited Thiis-Evensen to lecture on Postmodernism. Anticipating a skeptical audience, Thiis-Evensen nonetheless planned to expound on his belief that Postmodernism has to do with the character of space. Where Modernism emphasizes the openness of spaces flowing from one to another, Postmodernism is marked by more closed, individual spaces. Where Modernism emphasizes the honest expression of a structure, Postmodernism emphasizes building masses. And although the forms associated with American Postmodernism have typically recalled classical forms, Thiis-Evensen believes this restriction will liberalize and evolve into a fresh aesthetic vocabulary.

Many church architects in Europe, including Thiis-Evensen, are practicing Postmodernism under its broad definition, sometimes without knowing it and more often without admitting it. Frequently, for example, an architect is called upon both to preserve part of an existing and perhaps historic religious structure, such as a bell tower or an apse, and to design a new structure that expands the worship space and support facilities. These requirements demand an exploration of how historical forms can inspire compatible, contemporary forms or be adapted in a fresh manner. Postmodernism, as it is known in the United States, is often characterized by façades that recall historical forms. In Europe, the need for such imagery may be even greater because of the historical context of architecture and civilization there.

Many architects are successfully addressing the tension between old and new, between historical and contemporary. In the design of a new church surrounding a historic bell tower in Hövelhof, West Germany, architect J. G. Hanke masterfully—and respectfully—manipulates forms, materials, and colors in a way that is fresh, but not "Modern." At the Catholic Kirche St. Michael in Ummeln and Kirche Liebfrauen in Jöllenbeck, both near Bielefeld, architect Hanke has designed equally fresh and sensitive alterations to older structures. None of his designs could be labeled Modern, and Postmodern may be too extreme a tag. Hanke's work defies absolute categorization; undoubtedly, that contributes to its success. Whether Hanke and others like him know it—or will admit it—they have begun to throw away the "rules" of the Modern movement and are, if not yet practicing Postmodernism, at least leading the transition in that direction.

*Fresh, but not Modern, the 1979
church surrounds a historic bell tower,
leaving the interior to appear at once
old and new. Kirche St. Johannes
Nepomuk, Hövelhof, West Germany.*

Kirche St. Michael,
Ummeln, West Germany.

Stylistic attempts to mimic history without due respect are met with disdain by European architects. Their suspicion of Postmodernism stems from their exposure to American exercises that sometimes cleverly interpret historical forms, but are all too often seen as humorous mockeries of the classics. At Neviges and Wigratzbad, West Germany, noted architect Gottfried Böhm has produced powerful new churches in the contexts of old, historic villages. These projects are clearly departures from the Modern movement. Yet, when asked if he considered his work to exemplify Postmodernism in Germany, Böhm flatly stated, "I am not an 'ism!'" Another German architect, Manfred Ludes, gives the American Postmodern movement credit for forcing him and his colleagues to reexamine their work and find fresh approaches to design. But to Ludes, Postmodernism has gone too far and is impractical. "It's okay to look at," he says, "but not to build!" Inger and Johannes Exner are even more critical of the current trend. They cite projects in which "the exterior is given some unusual, exciting form, to which exaggerated and functionally superfluous architectural refinements are added." Instead, in their work for the Lutheran Church, they design in the belief that "the exterior should be of demonstratively simple, unostentatious form, which many will perhaps think boring or ugly, but which in its essence tries to clarify the Protestant church building."

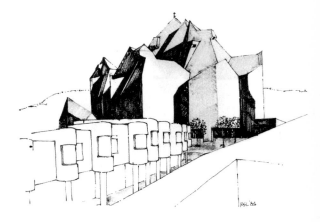

Powerful new church in an old village clearly departs from the Modern movement. Wallfahrtskirche Maria Königin des Friedens, Neviges, West Germany.

In the United States, architects are usually selected by interview, with the client using as criteria a candidate's experience, reputation, and ability to meet schedule and budget restrictions. In Europe, the selection process is dominated by competitions. Most new churches in Europe began as winning entries in design competitions. In a typical competition, architects from the local area, and often from the entire country, are provided with a statement of needs and invited to submit their designs for the proposed new church. Then a committee, which might include ministers, priests, laypeople, and other architects, selects the winner, usually without having had any prior communication with the participating architects. Some contend that this process puts appropriate focus on the architects' design abilities, and therefore elevates aesthetic quality. Others, who see the design process as a team effort, say that competitions deprive the architect of the most valuable team-member during design—the client. Stuttgart architect Wilfried Beck-Erlang accurately describes the competition process: "You have no partners in the first stages of the project—no priest, no church members.

According to the architects, "a demonstratively simple, unostentatious form that tries to clarify the Protestant church building." Sædden Kirke, Esbjerg, Denmark.

You must be a detective!" As a result, the winning solution may not always be the best solution. The new church in Waldweiler, West Germany—the one referred to by townspeople as the "Holy Jail"— was the winning solution in a design competition, but was obviously not the solution that might have been produced had church members been more closely involved in the decision-making process.

The "Holy Jail" was designed by Heinz Bienefeld of Swisttal, West Germany, and, judging from his comments, he may be among those who actually prefer the competition process. He laments that new churches could be so much better were building committees to insist on higher levels of design. Recalling his experiences, he observes that "people responsible for building churches prefer second- or third-class architecture. They like 'living room' design. A first-class architect will quickly come to confrontation with a building committee, but a second- or third-class architect gives them what they want and has no problem with them."

In an attempt to avoid the situation that Bienefeld describes, Inger and Johannes Exner have occasionally turned the tables on their prospective clients, interviewing *them* to see if the committee is qualified. The Exners examine each issue of design for its meaning to the church, and they expect the building committee to do the same. Once, when invited to design a new church, the Exners met for the first time with a committee of church members and boldly asked if the committee knew anything about church design. When it became obvious that the answer was "relatively little," the architects provided each committee member with reading material, suggested additional methods of study, and told the committee that they would talk again in about a year. One year later, the Exners met with a much more sophisticated client and embarked together on a very successful design experience. The Exners are quick to acknowledge, however, that with so bold an approach, "You can sometimes lose a client!"

Like many European churches, the "Holy Jail" was the winner of a design competition but conceived without parish input. Kirche in Waldweiler, Waldweiler, West Germany.

127

Land of Oz or House of God?

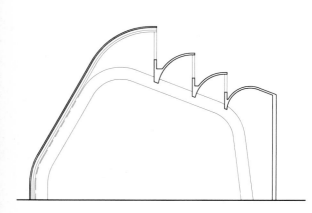

Forms to capture light: a colleague calls it a "giant reflector," but visitors know it as the "Church of Alvar Aalto." Chiesa di Santa Maria Assunta, Riola, Italy.

Europe's churchbuilders—building committees, priests, ministers, neighbors, city officials, and architects—all share in the responsibility for new church design, but do they still believe in God? Aalto's protégé, Tide Huesser, asserts that ancient cathedrals "were built when people still believed in God! Today, churches are just aesthetics, built to create jobs and spend church-tax monies." He goes on to suggest that Aalto himself was not a very religious man, that he believed more strongly in humankind. Huesser's remarks may be speculative or even unfair, but the last church Aalto designed before his death holds an interesting irony. The great Finnish architect practically worshipped Italy, and finally, in his later years, he was asked to design a church for the small village of Riola, near Bologna. The Italians there thought as much of Aalto as he thought of them. He died during the construction of the Riola church, never seeing it completed, and as if to grant martyrdom to the fallen architect, the Italians named the plaza in front of the church Piazza del Alvar Aalto. Today, long after Aalto's death, visitors to the church buy picture postcards of the striking edifice. Nowhere on the cards can be found the name of the church, but prominently, in four languages, appears the description, "Church of Alvar Aalto."

Is Riola's church a House of God or a House of Aalto? Huesser's comments imply that new churches are not unlike L. Frank Baum's fictional Land of Oz—"just aesthetics," just elaborate structures, costumes, and mystery. In the conclusion of Baum's metaphorical tale, the Wizard of Oz turns out to be no more than a powerless phony. Or does he? In fact, he is actually powerful enough to make Dorothy, the Scarecrow, the Tin Man, and the Cowardly Lion realize that they can find what they seek and explain what cannot be explained simply by believing. Some would call that "faith."

Do Europe's churchbuilders still believe in God? Throughout the world, churches are as varied as the people who build them, just as the world's many concepts of God are as varied as the people who contemplate Him. If churches are built with the intent of scaring people into believing, then Huesser is correct—they are just aesthetics, just stage sets from which to sell a convincing story. But Huesser is not entirely correct. The new churches of Europe are more often products *of* faith than attempts to *sell* faith. A church building alone cannot convince anyone to become a believer, but it can provide an inspiring environment for those who do believe. In Europe, the people who build churches are still believers.

Appendix

Project Directory

Great Britain

Holy Innocents Catholic Church [1], Strickland Way, Orpington, Kent, BR6 9UE
Completed in 1981
1,004 square meters; 250 seats
Architect: Dr. Michael Blee; Michael Blee Design Partnership, Hill Lodge Studios, St. Annes Hill, Lewes BN7 1XY, Sussex, Great Britain
Clergy in 1984: The Very Reverend Canon John McNamara

The Ismaili Centre [2], Cromwell Gardens, South Kensington, London
Completed in 1983
6,500 square meters; 1,250 seats
Architect: Neville Conder, CBE, RIBA, FSIA, and Kenneth Price, RIBA; Casson Conder Partnership, Architects, 35 Thurloe Place, London SW7 2HJ, Great Britain

St. Margaret Church [3], St. Margaret's Road, East Twickenham, Middlesex
Completed in 1968
250 seats
Architect: Austin Winkley with Jaime Bellalta; Williams & Winkley Architects, 40 Linhope Street, London NW1 6HW, Great Britain
Clergy in 1984: The Very Reverend Canon D. Swan

All Saints Church Centre [4], Windsor
Completed in 1973
150 seats
Architect: Hutchison, Lock & Monk; Rayleigh House, 2 Richmond Hill, Richmond, Surrey TW10 6QX, Great Britain
Clergy in 1984: The Reverend J. A. Stone

St. Elphege's Church [5], Wallington
Completed in 1972
300 seats
Architect: Williams & Winkley Architects, 40 Linhope Street, London NW1 6HW, Great Britain
Clergy in 1984: The Reverend J. Mulholland

Christchurch United Reformed Church and Crown House Offices [6],
William Street, Windsor, Berkshire
Completed in 1980
Architect: Garnett Cloughley Blakemore and Associates
Clergy in 1984: The Reverend Ivy Halden, B.A.

Priory of Our Lady of Good Counsel [7], Sayers Common, Hassocks,
West Sussex BN6 9HT
Completed in 1978
3,550 square meters; 200 seats
Architect: Dr. Michael Blee; Michael Blee Design Partnership, Hill
Lodge Studios, St. Annes Hill, Lewes BN7 1XY, Sussex,
Great Britain
Clergy in 1984: Mother Mary Thomas

Isleworth Parish Church [8], Church Street, Isleworth
Completed in 1969
933 square meters; 250 seats
Architect: Dr. Michael Blee; Michael Blee Design Partnership, Hill
Lodge Studios, St. Annes Hill, Lewes BN7 1XY, Sussex,
Great Britain
Clergy in 1984: The Venerable Derek Hayward

Baptist Church and Youth Centre [9], South Circular Road, London
Completed in 1987
Architect: Dr. Michael Blee; Michael Blee Design Partnership, Hill
        Lodge Studios, St. Annes Hill, Lewes BN7 1XY, Sussex,
        Great Britain

Denmark

Gellerup Kirke [10], Gudrunsvej, Brabrand
Completed in 1976
400 square meters per floor; 400 seats (including balcony)
Architect: Knud Blach Petersen; Kystvejen 45, 8000 Århus C.,
        Denmark
Clergy in 1984: Jorgen Lasgaard

Avedøre Kirke [11], Traedrejerporten 6, Hvidovre (Avedøre
        Stationsby)
Completed in 1977
1,400 square meters; 220 seats
Architect: Palle Rydahl Drost, Arkitekt MAA; Lundtoftevej 1 C,
        DK-2800 Kgs. Lyngby, Denmark
Clergy in 1984: Niels Kristensen

Bagsværd Kirke [12], Taxvej 16, Bagsværd
Completed in 1976
Architect: Jørn Utzon

Sædden Kirke [13], Fyrvej 30, 6710 Esbjerg V
Completed in 1978
484 square meters (church only), 1,540 square meters total; 500
        seats (including balcony)
Architect: Inger og Johannes Exner; Marselisvej 19, 8000 Århus C.,
        Denmark
Clergy in 1984: Bennet Østergaard and Gertrud Bisgaard

Gug Kirke [14], Byplanvej, Gug, Ålborg
Completed in 1972
910 square meters; 120 seats plus 90 in overflow
Architect: Inger og Johannes Exner; Marselisvej 19, 8000 Århus C.,
        Denmark

Islev Kirke [15], Slotsherrensvej 321, 2610 Rødovre
Completed in 1970
341 square meters (church only), 1,237 square meters total; 200
    seats plus 130 in overflow
Architect: Inger og Johannes Exner; Marselisvej 19, 8000 Århus C.,
    Denmark
Clergy in 1984: Eric Linneboe

Ellevang Kirke [16], Jellebakken 42, 8240 Risskov
Completed in 1974
946 square meters; 200 seats
Architect: Friis og Moltke; Vesterbrogade 32, 8000 Århus C,
    Denmark
Clergy in 1984: Kjeld Holm and Gyrite Danielsen

Ravnsbjergkirken [17], Grofthøjparken 1, Århus, Viby
Completed in 1976
1,075 square meters; 225 seats
Architect: Arkitektfirmaet C. F. Møllers Tegnestue, Mads Møller;
    Kriegersvej 31, 8000 Århus C, Denmark
Clergy in 1984: Aage Andersen

Opstandelseskirken [18], Gymnasievej 2, DK-2620 Albertslund
Completed in 1984
200 square meters (church only), 1,274 square meters total; 75 seats
    plus 75 in overflow
Architect: Inger og Johannes Exner; Marselisvej 19, 8000 Århus C.,
    Denmark
Clergy in 1984: Poul Exner

Finland

Malmin Kirkko [19], Malmi (Helsinki)
Completed in 1981
Architect: Kristian Gullichsen

Ristin Kirkko [20], Kolkanmaki Hill, Lahti
Completed in 1978
1,200 seats
Architect: Alvar Aalto; Arkkitehtitoimisto Alvar Aalto & Co., Tiili-
        maki 20, 00330 Helsinki 33, Finland
Project Architects: Marjata Kivijärvi and Tide Huesser

Vuosaari Kirkko [21] Satamasaarentie 7, 00980 Helsinki
Completed in 1980
1,570 square meters; 270 seats plus 220 in overflow
Architect: Arkkitehtitoimisto Pirkko ja Arvi Ilonen; Hiihtäjäntie 8
        B1, 00810 Helsinki 81, Finland
Clergy in 1984: Yrjö Karanko

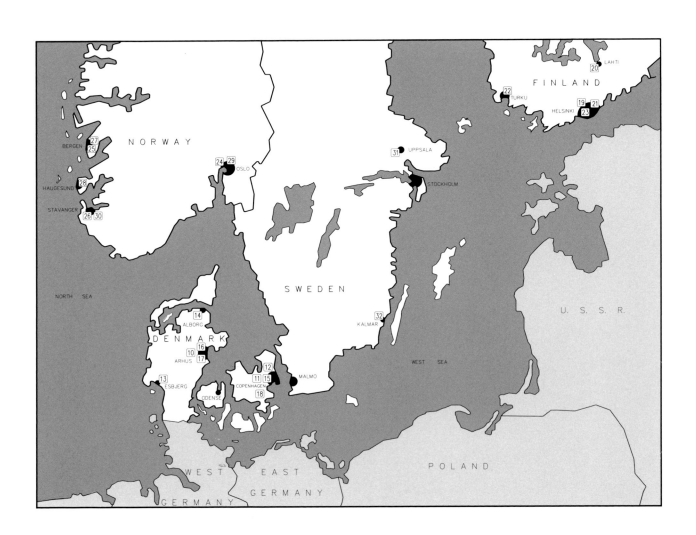

Henrikin Kirkko [22], Turku
Completed in 1980
1,490 square meters, 450 seats
Architect: Arkkitehtitoimisto Pitkänen, Laiho & Raunio, Kauppias-
    katu 4B, 20100 Turku, Finland
Clergy in 1984: Esko Thurén

Temppeliaukion Kirkko [23], Lutherinkatu 3, 00100 Helsinki
Completed in 1969
1,790 square meters; 940 seats
Architect: Timo ja Tuomo Suomalainen; Itäranta 7, 02110 Espoo
    11, Finland
Clergy in 1984: Pauli Vuola

Norway

Østerås Kirke [24], Baerum (Oslo)
Completed in 1974
Architect: Ashish Krishna og Viggo Kippenes, Norway

Søreide Kirke [25], 5060 Søreidgrend, Bergen
Completed in 1973.
1,370 square meters; 305 seats
Architect: Helge Hjertholm, Arkitekt MNAL; Østre Hopsvei 19B,
    5043 Hop, Norway
Clergy in 1984: Ragnar Gunnestad

Bekkefaret Kirke [26], Stavanger
Completed in 1977
1,695 square meters; 230 seats
Architect: Per Amund Riseng og Jan Stensrud, Arkiktekter MNAL,
    Akebergvn 56, Oslo 6, Norway
Clergy in 1984: Finn Gunnar Tonnesen

Eidsvåg Kirke [27], Vollane 3, N-5080 Eidsvåg i Åsane
Completed in 1982
1,700 square meters; 375 seats
Architect: Kjell Lund og Nils Slaatto, Arkiktekter MNAL; Bygdøy
    Allé 13, N-0257 Oslo 2, Norway
Clergy in 1984: Arne Brekke

Rossabø Kirke [28], Torvastad gt., Haugesund
Completed in 1972
1,620 square meters total; 376 seats plus 171 in overflow
Architect: Per Amund Riseng og Jan Stensrud, Arkiktekter MNAL;
        Akebergvn 56, Oslo 6, Norway
Clergy in 1984: Per Arnulv Nordboe

Østenstad Kirke [29], Gudolf Blakstadsvei 40, 1393 Østenstad
Completed in 1980
2,300 square meters; 350 seats plus 650 in overflow
Architect: Harald Hilles Arkitektkontor AS; Osterhausgaten 18,
        Oslo 1, Norway
Project Architects: Harald Hille, MNAL, and Tore Wiig, MNAL
Clergy in 1984: Thor Wagle

St. Svithun Katolske Kirke [30], Dronningens gate 10, Stavanger
Completed in 1983
230 square meters; 220 seats
Architect: Thomas Thiis-Evensen; Arkitekthøgskolen I Oslo, St.
        Olavs gt. 6, Postboks 6768 St. Olavs pl., 0165 Oslo 1,
        Norway
Clergy in 1984: Alexander Kors

Sweden

Gottsunda Kyrka [31], Uppsala
Completed in 1980
2,050 square meters; 310 seats plus 100 in overflow
Architect: Carl Nyren and Snorre Lindquist; Carl Nyren Arkitekt-
        kontor, Ferkens grand 3, Box 1250, S-111 82 Stockholm,
        Sweden
Clergy in 1984: Börje Jansson

Sankta Birgitta Kyrka [32], Kalmar
Completed in 1975
600 square meters (church only), 1,000 square meters total; 200
        seats
Architect: Ove Hidemark; Ove Hidemark/Göran Månsson Arki-
        tektkontor AB, Drottninggatan 59, 111 21 Stockholm,
        Sweden
Clergy in 1984: Anders Alberius

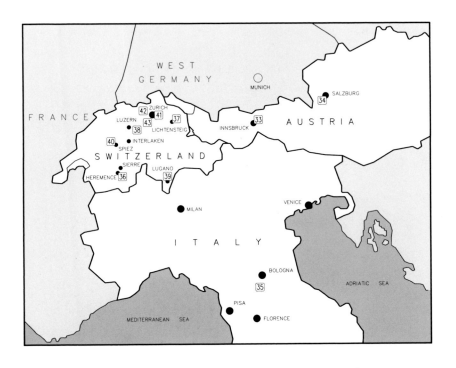

Austria

Pfarrzentrum Neu-Rum [33], Innsbruck
Completed in 1978
556 square meters; 350 seats
Architect: Dipl.-Ing. Horst Herbert Parson; Erzherzog-Eugen-
    strasse 3, 6060 Innsbruck, Austria
Clergy in 1984: Albert Markt

Kirche St. Vital [34], Salzburg
Architect: Wilhelm Holzbauer

Italy

Chiesa di Santa Maria Assunta [35], Riola
Completed in 1978
300 seats
Architect: Alvar Aalto; Arkkitehtitoimisto Alvar Aalto & Co., Tiili-
    maki 20, 00330 Helsinki 33, Finland
Project Architect: Vezio Nava
Clergy in 1984: Luigi Nuvoli

Switzerland

L'Église St. Nicolas d'Hérémence en Valais [36], Hérémence
Completed in 1971
550 seats
Architect: Prof. Walter M. Förderer; CH-8240 Thayngen,
    Switzerland
Clergy in 1984: Vanney

Kirche in Lichtensteig [37], Lichtensteig
Completed in 1968
500 seats
Architect: Prof. Walter M. Förderer; CH-8240 Thayngen,
    Switzerland

Agatha Kirche [38], CH-6033 Buchrain, Kt. Luzern Completed in
    1972
1,150 square meters; 450 seats
Architect: J. Naef + Prof. E. Studer + G. Studer, Architekten BSA
    AG; Zürich, Switzerland

Chiesa di Christo Risorto [39], Lugano
Completed in 1975
Architect: Rino Tami, Sorengo, Switzerland

Katholische Kirche Bruder Klaus [40], Belvédèrestrasse 6, Spiez
Completed in 1974
450 seats
Architect: Prof. Dr. Justus Dahinden; Architekturbüro, Kienasten-
    wiesweg 38, CH-8053 Zürich, Switzerland
Clergy in 1984: H. Blötzer

Maria Krönungskirche [41], Zürich-Witikon
Completed in 1965
500 seats
Architect: Prof. Dr. Justus Dahinden; Architekturbüro, Kienasten-
    wiesweg 38, CH-8053 Zürich, Switzerland
Clergy in 1984: Dr. Walter Blattmann

Katholische Kirche St. Antonius [42], Wildegg AG
Completed in 1970
1,600 square meters; 350 seats
Architect: Prof. Dr. Justus Dahinden; Architekturbüro, Kienasten-
    wiesweg 38, CH-8053 Zürich, Switzerland
Clergy in 1984: Katechet Bernet

Kirchliches Zentrum St. Johannes [43], Zug
Completed in 1971
Architect: I. Hafner, dipl. Arch. BSA/SIA, and A. Wiederkehr,
    Arch. SIA; Zug, Switzerland

West Germany

Katholische Kirchengemeinde Heiligkreuz [44], Schützenstrasse, 4270
    Altendorf-Ulfkotte
Completed in 1974
650 square meters; 350 seats
Architect: Dipl.-Ing. Manfred Ludes; Ludes Architektur- und Inge-
    nieurbüro, Heroldstrasse 26, 4270 Dorsten 21, West
    Germany
Clergy in 1984: Beike

Marienkirche [45], Benediktbeuern
550 square meters; 300 seats
Architect: Fritz Hierl; Stocket 10, 8110 Murnau, West Germany
Clergy in 1984: Johannes Mittermayer

Pfarrkirche Christi Auferstehung [46], Köln-Melaten
Completed in 1970
Architect: Dipl.-Ing. Architekt Prof. Gottfried Böhm, Architektur-
    büro Böhm, Auf Dem Römerberg 25, 5000 Köln 51 (Ma-
    rienburg), West Germany

Pfarrkirche St. Anna [47], Ascheberg-Davensberg
Completed in 1976
727 square meters; 330 seats
Architect: Dipl.-Ing. Manfred Ludes, Ludes Architektur- und Inge-
    nieurbüro, Heroldstrasse 26, 4270 Dorsten 21, West
    Germany
Clergy in 1984: Berkenbusch and Ulrich Koch

Franziskanerkloster [48], Lippestrasse-Klosterstrasse-Westgraben, 4270 Dorsten
Completed in 1980
274 square meters; 180 seats
Architect: Dipl.-Ing. Manfred Ludes, Ludes Architektur- und Ingenieurbüro, Heroldstrasse 26, 4270 Dorsten 21, West Germany
Clergy in 1984: Wilfried

Gemeindezentrum St. Aloysius [49], Altendernerstrasse 69, 4600 Dortmund-Derne
Completed in 1978
425 square meters; 300 seats
Architect: J. G. Hanke, Architekt BDA; Tümmlerweg 21, 4800 Bielefeld 16, West Germany
Clergy in 1984: Jostmeier

Pfarrkirche St. Stephanus [50], 4423 Gescher-Hochmoor
Completed in 1976
516 square meters; 280 seats
Architect: Dipl.-Ing. Manfred Ludes, Ludes Architektur- und Ingenieurbüro, Heroldstrasse 26, 4270 Dorsten 21, West Germany
Clergy in 1984: Rensing

Katholische Kirche der Gemeinde Litzelstetten [51], Konstanz-Litzelstetten
Completed in 1978
Architect: Herbert Schaudt; Schaudt Freier Architekt, BDA, dwb; Seestrasse 1, 7750 Konstanz, West Germany

Pfarrkirche St. Jakobus [52], Limburg-Lindenholzhausen
Completed in 1979.
1,000 square meters; 310 seats
Architect: Prof. Dr. Justus Dahinden, Kienastenwiesweg 38, Architekturbüro, CH-8053 Zürich, Switzerland
Clergy in 1984: Willy Siegmund

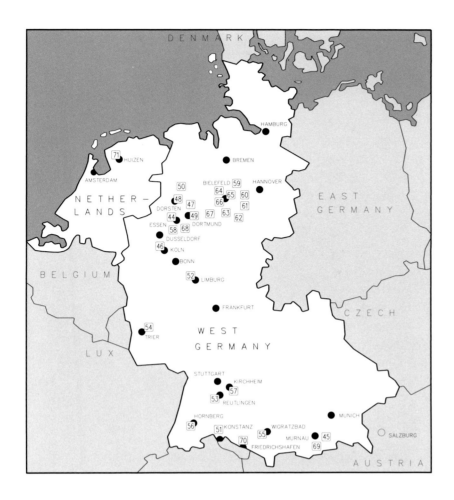

Kirche St. Andreas [53], Reutlingen-Orschelhagen
Completed in 1969
500 seats
Architect: Dipl.-Ing. Wilfried Beck-Erlang, Architektenbüro Beck-
    Erlang, Planckstrasse 60, Stuttgart 1, West Germany
Clergy in 1984: Richard Kappler

Kirche in Waldweiler [54], Hauptstrasse, Waldweiler
Completed in 1976
950 square meters; 550 seats
Architect: Heinz Bienefeld, Architekt BDA; Haus Derkum, 5357
    Swisttal-Ollheim, West Germany
Clergy in 1984: Jakobs

Herz-Jesu- und Maria Sühnekirche [55], 8996 Wigratzbad
Completed in 1975
Architect: Dipl.-Ing. Architekt Prof. Gottfried Böhm; Architektur-
    büro Böhm, Auf Dem Römerberg 25, 5000 Köln 59 (Ma-
    rienburg), West Germany

Kirche St. Johannes der Täufer [56], Reichenbacherstrasse 9, 7746
    Hornberg-Schwarzwald
Completed in 1972
900 square meters; 600 seats
Architect: Dipl.-Ing. Rainer Disse, Karlsruhe-Waldstatt, West
    Germany
Clergy in 1984: Karl Schludi

Hochbauten Wald-Friedhof [57], 7312 Kirchheim-Teck
Completed in 1979
810 square meters; 230 seats
Architect: P. M. Kaufmann, Freier Architekt BDA, 7440 Nürtin-
    gen-Oberensingen, West Germany
Clergy in 1984: Käser

Wallfahrtskirche Maria, Königin des Friedens [58], 5620 Velbert 15
    (Neviges)
Completed in 1968
Architect: Dipl.-Ing. Architekt Prof. Gottfried Böhm; Architektur-
    büro Böhm, Auf Dem Römerberg 25, 5000 Köln 59 (Ma-
    rienburg), West Germany

Katholische Kirche St. Joseph [59], Phillippstrasse 3, 4980 Bünde 1
Completed in 1967
765 square meters; 500 seats
Architect: J. G. Hanke, Architekt BDA; Tümmlerweg 21, 4800
    Bielefeld 16, West Germany
Clergy in 1984: Hellweg

Katholische Kirche Heiliggeist [60], Pideritstrasse 12, 4920 Lemgo
Completed in 1967
685 square meters; 550 seats
Architect: J. G. Hanke, Architekt BDA; Tümmlerweg 21, 4800
    Bielefeld 16, West Germany
Clergy in 1984: Menzel

Katholische Kirche Zu Allen Heiligen [61], Berlebeck
Completed in 1966
515 square meters; 275 seats
Architect: J. G. Hanke, Architekt BDA; Tümmlerweg 21, 4800
    Bielefeld 16, West Germany
Clergy in 1984: Jacobs

Katholische Kirche St. Kilian [62], Gertrudenstrasse 14, 4790
    Paderborn
Completed in 1967
985 square meters; 500 seats
Architect: J. G. Hanke, Architekt BDA; Tümmlerweg 21, 4800
    Bielefeld 16, West Germany
Clergy in 1984: Mathei

Katholische Kirche St. Johannes Nepomuk und Pfarrheim [63], Schloss-
    strasse 9, 4791 Hövelhof
Completed in 1979
1,225 square meters; 600 seats
Architect: J. G. Hanke, Architekt BDA; Tümmlerweg 21, 4800
    Bielefeld 16, West Germany
Clergy in 1984: Heller

Katholische Kirche Liebfrauen [64], Wordstrasse 5, 4800 Bielefeld 15
    (Jöllenbeck)
Completed in 1984
390 square meters; 190 seats
Architect: J. G. Hanke, Architekt BDA; Tümmlerweg 21, 4800
    Bielefeld 16, West Germany
Clergy in 1984: Dechant Algermissen

Katholische Kirche St. Michael und Pfarrheim [65], Am Depenbrocks-
    hof 39, 4800 Bielefeld 14 (Ummeln)
Completed in 1983
390 square meters; 200 seats
Architect: J. G. Hanke, Architekt BDA; Tümmlerweg 21, 4800
    Bielefeld 16, West Germany
Clergy in 1984: Balsfulland

Katholische Kirche Bruder Konrad Spexard und Pfarrheim [66], Bonifa-
    tiusstrasse 2, 4830 Gütersloh
Completed in 1974
745 square meters; 495 seats
Architect: J. G. Hanke, Architekt BDA; Tümmlerweg 21, 4800
    Bielefeld 16, West Germany
Clergy in 1984: Davits

Katholische Kirche Bonifatius und Pfarrheim [67], Pappelallee, 4780
    Lippstadt
Completed in 1978
450 square meters; 260 seats
Architect: J. G. Hanke, Architekt BDA; Tümmlerweg 21, 4800
    Bielefeld 16, West Germany
Clergy in 1984: Kathke

Filialkirche St. Matthias und Evangelisches Gemeindezentrum [68], Auf
    der Höhe, Kettwig
Completed in 1980
Architect: Dipl.-Ing. Architekt Prof. Gottfried Böhm; Architektur-
    büro Böhm, Auf Dem Römerberg 25, 5000 Köln 51 (Ma-
    rienburg), West Germany

Filialkirche St. George [69], Grossweil
Completed in 1962
400 square meters; 260 seats
Architect: Fritz Hierl; Stocket 10, 8110 Murnau, West Germany
Clergy in 1984: Josef Stadler

Kirche Der Gute Hirte [70], Friedrichshafen-Nord (Bodensee)
Completed in 1969
500 seats
Architect: Dipl.-Ing. Wilfried Beck-Erlang; Architektenbüro Beck-
    Erlang, Planckstrasse 60, Stuttgart 1, West Germany
Clergy in 1984: Hans Maier

Netherlands

Gereformeerde Kerk De Akker [71], Gooierserf 99, Huizen
Completed in 1979
510 square meters; 250 seats plus 350 in overflow
Architect: Zuiderhoek; Baarn, Netherlands
Clergy in 1984: Ds. W. v. Wieren

Bibliography

"Aalto in Italy." *Progressive Architecture* 60, No. 3 (May 1979): 57–63.

"Alvar Aalto in Italia: la Chiesa di Riola." *Domus*, No. 587 (October 1978): 8–13.

Architectural Guide Switzerland. Ed. Florian Adler, et al. Zürich: Les Editions d'Architecture Artemis, 1969–1978.

"Avedøre Kirke." *Arkitektur (DK)* 27, No. 4 (July 1983): 165–169.

"Bagsværd Kirke." *Arkitektur (DK)* 26, No. 3 (May 1982): 81–91.

Blaser, Werner. *Architecture 70/80 Switzerland*. Basel: Birkhauser Verlag, 1982.

"Bekkefaret Kirke." *Byggekunst* 59, No. 5 (1977): 154–157.

"Beton Sacre: Professor Förderer's Swiss Churches." *Concrete Quarterly*, No. 98.

"Bruder-Klaus-Kirche in Spiez/CH." *Deutsche Bauzeitschrift* 25, No. 3 (March 1977).

"Chiesa di Cristo Risorto a Melaten, Colonia, 1966–68." *L'Architettura, Cron E Storia* 19, No. 12 (April 1974): 718–738.

"Chiesa a Lugano." *L'Architettura, Cron E Storia* 22, No. 7 (253) (November 1976): 372–377.

"Church Defensive?" *Architects Journal* 714, No. 37 (September 1981): 528–531.

Clouten, Neville. "Perinteisen ja uuden rinnastuksia." *Arkkitehti* 80, No. 4 (1983): 44–47.

"Dahinden in Lindenholzhausen." *Architectural Review* 170, No. 1014 (August 1981): 72–73.

"Datid Och Nutid I Samma Hand." *Arkitektur* (Stockholm) 78, No. 9 (1978): 2–27.

Davies, J. C., *Temples, Churches and Mosques*. Oxford: Basil Blackwell Publisher Limited, 1982.

"Eidsvåg Kirke." *Byggekunst* 65, No. 5 (May 1983): 210–215.

"Election '84." *Time* 124, No. 21 (November 19, 1984): 36.

"Ellevang Kirke, Vejlby." *Arkitektur (DK)* 22, No. 2 (1978): 56–63.

Exner, J. and Christiansen, Tage. *Kirkebygning og Teologi*. Kobenhavn: G. E. C. Gads Forlag, 1965.

"Franziskanerkloster in Dorsten." *Deutsche Bauzeitschrift* 28, No. 4 (April 1980): 515–518.

"Gellerup Kirke, Brabrand." *Arkitektur (DK)* 21, No. 6 (1977): 242–248.

"Gemeindezentrum, Kirche, Kindergarten in Dortmund." *Deutsche Bauzeitschrift* 28, No. 12 (December 1980): 1811–1814.

"Gereformeerde Kerk in Huizen." *Bouw* 35, No. 22 (October 25, 1980): 78–79.

"God and Mammon." *Building* 239, No. 7169 (50) (December 12, 1980): 31–38.

"Gug Kirke." *Arkitektur (DK)* 19, No. 4 (1975): 125–131.

"Henrikin Kirkko." *Arkkitehti* 77, No. 8 (1980): 18–21, 58–59.

"Hochbauten Waldfriedhof Kirchheim/Teck." *Deutsche Bauzeitschrift*, No. 4 (April 1980): 523–524.

"Innkeeping: A Boon for the Wirsthaus." *Time* 124, No. 24 (December 10, 1984): 65.

"Islamic Architecture Turns to Modern and Traditional Designs." *Building* 237, No. 7105 (September 14, 1979): 16.

"Islev Kirke." *Arkitektur (DK)* 17, No. 5 (1973): 187–195.

"Katholische Pfarrkirche St. Stephanus in Gescher-Hochmoor." *Deutsche Bauzeitschrift* 25, No. 11 (November 1977): 1447–1448.

"Katholische Pfarrkirche St. Anna in Davensberg." *Deutsche Bauzeitschrift* 25, No. 11 (November 1977): 1449–1450.

"Katholische Kirche in Buchrain, Kanton Luzern." *Deutsche Bauzeitschrift* 22, No. 7 (July 1974): 1248.

"Katholische Kirche St. Andreas in Reutlingen/Orschel-Hagen." *Deutsche Bauzeitschrift* 22, No. 7 (July 1974): 1250.

"Katholische Gemeindezentrum und Terrassenhäuser in Hornberg." *Deutsche Bauzeitschrift*, No. 7 (July 1974).

"Katholische Kirche in Konstanz-Litzelstetten." *Werk, Bauen & Wohnen* 67/34, No. 10 (October 1980): 38–40.

"Kirche in Konstanz-Litzelstetten." *Baumeister* 77, No. 1: 60–63.

"Kirche in Waldweiler." *Baumeister* 77, No. 1: 53–55.

"L'Eglise St. Margaret A East Twickenham." *Art D'Eglise* 46, No. 182 (January 1978): 233–236.

"L'Eglise Saint-Vital A Salzbourg." *Art D'Eglise* 45, No. 178 (January 1977): 112–116.

"L'Eglise de Waldweiler." *Art D'Eglise* 45, No. 178 (January 1977): 105–111.

"L'Eglise Saint-Elphege A Wallington." *Art D'Eglise* 46, No. 182 (January 1978): 229–232.

"Malmin Kirkko." *Arkkitehti* 80, No. 4 (1983): 28–33.

"Østenstad Kirke." *Byggekunst* 65, No. 6 (May 1983): 219–221.

"Østerås Kirke." *Byggekunst* 57, No. 6 (1975): 146–149.

"Parish Center, Innsbruck." *Architectural Review* 165, No. 987 (May 1979): 290–292.

"Pfarrkirche des Dorfes Benediktbeuern." *Detail*, No. 2 (March 1981): 176–180.

"Pfarrkirche in Altendorf-Ulfkotte." *Deutsche Bauzeitschrift* 22, No. 7 (July 1974): 1249.

"Pfarrzentrum Neu-Rum, Innsbruck." *Baumeister* 77, No. 1 (1980): 56–60.

"Ravnsbjergkirken, Viby." *Arkitektur (DK)* 21, No. 3 (1977): 89–98.

"Religious Centre." *RIBA Journal* 88, No. 3 (March 1981): 54.

"Ringing the Changes in Church Design." *RIBA Journal* 86, No. 12 (December 1979): 521–525.

"Ristin Kirkko." *Arkkitehti* 76, No. 5/6 (1979): 905–907.

"Rossabø Kirke." *Byggekunst* 65, No. 5 (May 1983): 216–218.

"Sædden Kirke." *Arkitektur (DK)* 26, No. 3 (May 1982): 92–97.

Schultz, Gisela, and Werner, Frank. *Beck-Erlang*. Stuttgart: Verlag Gerd Hatje, 1983.

"Søreide Kirke." *Byggekunst* 57, No. 6 (1975): 142–145.

"St. Elphege's Wallington, Surrey: Roman Catholic Church and Parish Complex." *Architects Journal* 158, No. 50 (December 12, 1973): 1469–1473.

"St. Svithun Katolske Kirke." *Byggekunst*, 223–237.

"Stahlbau Konstruktionen." *Detail*, No. 5 (September 1976): 635–638.

Treib, Marc. "Clouds of Concrete." *Progressive Architecture* 61, No. 9 (September 1980): 165–169.

"Utzon at Bagsværd." *Architectural Review* 165, No. 985 (March 1979): 146–149.

"Vuosaaren Kirkko." *Arkkitehti* 80, No. 4 (1983): 34–39.

"What is a Church?" *Architects Journal* 170, No. 30 (July 1979): 172–173.

Zanker, Alfred. "If You Think Your Taxes Are High." *U.S. News & World Report* 99, No. 12 (September 16, 1985): 51.

Index

Acknowledgments

Like the practice of architecture itself, this book is the product of so many minds and hands—a team of people who played direct and indirect roles, but who were all integral to the outcome. My thanks to each of them!

Without the generosity of Francis J. Plym—and the sustained vision of his son, Lawrence J. Plym—the University of Illinois would be without the prestigious Plym Traveling Fellowship, I would have been without the initial stimulus to conduct this investigation, and the new churches of Europe would still be largely unknown in America. Alan Forrester, Plym administrator and director of the School of Architecture, has extended his support from the beginning of this endeavor.

An architect's lifeblood comes from clients and colleagues, the people who make this profession so exciting and rewarding. Several of each supported my nomination for the Plym Fellowship and contributed to its success—Robert L. Curtis, James A. Tracy, C. Steven Sjogren, Jack Francis, Alvin R. (John) Harris, James R. Nelson, FAIA, Donald J. Hackl, FAIA, J. Eric Anderson, AIA, and a special colleague, role model, and friend, Lawrence B. Perkins, FAIA. Their support, and that of so many others who have followed, continues to inspire and motivate.

In Europe, architects at every location were abundantly generous with their time, assistance, courtesies, and kindness. I may criticize certain facets and features of some of their churches (without that this book would be neutered) but, taken as a whole, I am moved by the quality of their work, proud of my European colleagues, and delighted to have made many new friends among them. We American architects stand to learn much from them!

Clergymen at each church were obviously proud of their facilities, as evidenced by their eager willingness to share information, anecdotes, hospitality—and a great deal of coffee. Professional societies (each country's equivalent of the AIA) were immensely helpful in identifying architects, projects, and their locations.

Since 1974, I have been blessed with a second family, this one French. When travels take me to Versailles or the Pays-Basque region of France—as they did while I was traversing the Continent in search of new churches—I have a home. My gratitude goes to the entire Dufourcq family. The Overseas Division of the University of Illinois School of Architecture at Versailles, France, has also been "home" to me—first as a student, now as an alumnus. The leader of that 20-year-old program has been my teacher, adviser, motivator,